GCSE English

Great Expectations

by Charles Dickens

Great Expectations is a wonderful book — but writing GCSE essays about it is tougher than Miss Havisham's wedding cake.

Not to worry. This brilliant Text Guide explains the whole thing — characters, language, themes, historical background... the lot. And because it's a CGP book, we get straight to the point, with no needless rambling.

We've also included plenty of practice questions to test you on what you've learned, plus advice on how to plan and write top-grade answers in the exam! It's good enough to make even Estella smile. A bit.

The Text Guide

CONTENTS

Introduction

Section One — Background and Context

Section Two — Discussion of Chapters

CONTENTS

Section Three — Characters

Section Four — Themes

Section Five — The Writer's Techniques

Section Six — Exam Advice

Published by CGP

Editors:
Emma Crighton
Josephine Gibbons
Rachael Powers
Caley Simpson
Rebecca Tate

Contributors:
Holly Corfield-Carr
Jennifer Mannion
Angela Taylor

With thanks to Glenn Rogers, John Sanders and Jennifer Underwood for the proofreading

Acknowledgements:
Cover Illustration; Autumn Morning by Grimshaw, John Atkinson (1836-93) Private Collection/ © Mallett Gallery, London, UK/ The Bridgeman Art Library

With thanks to Gerry Murray for permission to use the photographs on pages 4, 5 & 25. Gerry Murray/Library Theatre Company, Manchester

With thanks to Rex Features for permission to use the images on pages 3, 4, 5, 13, 14, 15, 16, 19, 22, 26, 31, 34, 40, 43, 44, 45, 49, 56, 57 & 58

With thanks to Alamy for permission to use the images on pages 3 & 12

With thanks to akg-images for permission to use the images on pages 23 & 55

With thanks to TopFoto for permission to use the images on pages 20, 24 & 33 © TopFoto

With thanks to The Moviestore Collection for permission to use the images on pages 11, 17, 18, 32, 48, 52 & 53

With thanks to Mary Evans Picture Library for permission to use the images on pages 1, 2, 6, 7, 8 & 9

Image on page 1: Wentworth Street - Whitechapel, from 'London, a Pilgrimage', written by William Blanchard Jerrold (1826-84) & engraved by A. Bertrand, pub. 1872 (engraving) by Dore, Gustave (1832-83) Private Collection/ The Stapleton Collection/ The Bridgeman Art Library

Photos on pages 4 & 5 are of the Northern Stage Theatre Production of Great Expectations © Keith Pattison

With thanks to Robert Brookes (www.photos4all.co.uk) for permission to use the photographs on pages 3, 27, 30, 36, 37, 38, 46, 47 & 54, photos are of the Common Ground Theatre Company production of Great Expectations

ISBN: 978 1 84762 486 4
Printed by Elanders Ltd, Newcastle upon Tyne.
Clipart from Corel®

Based on the classic CGP style created by Richard Parsons.

Introduction to 'Great Expectations' and Dickens

'Great Expectations' is about growing up

- *Great Expectations* is about what happens to <u>Pip</u>, a poor boy, when he's given a large amount of <u>money</u>.

- Although the novel is <u>fictional</u>, it's based on Dickens' experiences of growing up in <u>19th century</u> Britain.

Social Class in 19th Century Britain

1) During the Industrial Revolution (see p.6), it became <u>easier</u> for people to improve their <u>social class</u> through <u>hard work</u>.

2) But there were still huge divisions in Britain's strict <u>class system</u>. Poor people lived in <u>terrible conditions</u> while the rich enjoyed <u>luxuries</u>.

3) There was also a lot of <u>class snobbery</u> — many upper class people looked down on anyone who hadn't <u>inherited</u> their wealth.

A nineteenth-century slum in London

Charles Dickens was interested in social change

- Dickens' family was <u>middle class</u>, but he also knew what it was like to be <u>poor</u>. When Dickens was twelve, his father was <u>imprisoned</u> for debt. The family was very poor and Dickens had to work in a <u>factory</u>.

- Dickens' experience of <u>poverty</u> made him very <u>critical</u> of the <u>class system</u>. <u>Social class</u> is one of the <u>main themes</u> of *Great Expectations*.

1812	<u>Born</u> on 7th February, in <u>Portsmouth</u>.
1824	His father is <u>arrested for debt</u> and sent to <u>prison</u>. Dickens has to give up his education and work in a <u>factory</u>.
1824-27	His father <u>inherits</u> some money so Dickens goes to <u>private school</u> for two years.
1827	Works as an office boy at a <u>solicitor's firm</u>.
1828	Starts work as a <u>court reporter</u>.
1833	<u>First short story</u> published — 'A Dinner at Poplar Walk'.
1836	<u>Marries</u> Catherine Hogarth.
1836-37	His first novel '<u>Pickwick Papers</u>' is serialised.
1860-61	'<u>Great Expectations</u>' is serialised.
1870	<u>Dies</u> of a stroke on 9th June. Buried in <u>Westminster Abbey</u>.

© Mary Evans Picture Library

2

Background Information

The novel is set in a village in Kent, and also in London

Here's a map of the main locations in the novel:

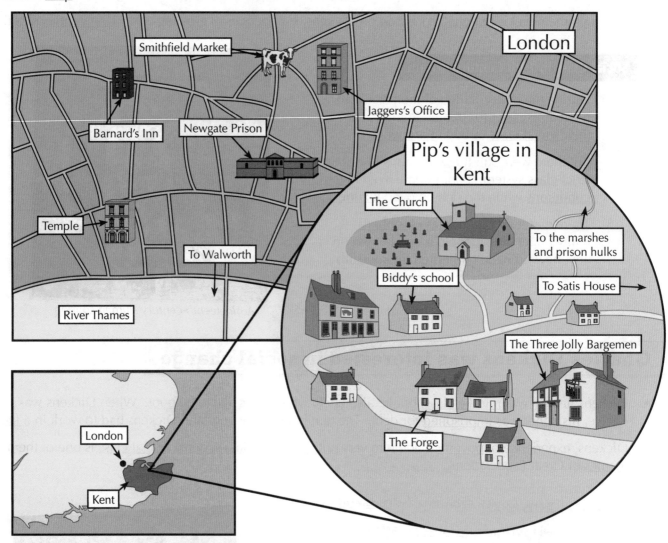

Life in the early 1800s was tough

The Seven Dials slum in London, 1850.

- The novel is set in the early 19th century, a time of social upheaval and huge changes. Although a few people became very wealthy, many more lived and worked in terrible conditions.

- There were some schools, but many families couldn't afford to send their children to be educated. Poor children had to get jobs instead.

- The laws were very harsh. People who committed relatively minor crimes could be sentenced to death or transportation (being sent to Australia). Prisons were overcrowded so the government had to keep some criminals on large boats called hulks instead.

Who's Who in 'Great Expectations'

Pip (Philip Pirrip)...

...is an orphan, the hero and the narrator. He dreams of being a gentleman, and is in love with Estella.

Estella...

...is Miss Havisham's adopted daughter. She's beautiful, but cruel to Pip.

Joe Gargery...

...is a kind blacksmith and Pip's brother-in-law, but is like a father to him.

Miss Havisham...

...is a rich, bitter old lady. She's never recovered from being jilted on her wedding day.

Mrs Joe...

...is Pip's older sister and Joe's wife. She's hot-tempered and cruel to Pip.

Herbert Pocket...

...is related to Miss Havisham. He and Pip fight as children but become friends in London.

Magwitch (or Provis)...

...is a criminal who forces Pip to steal food for him. He is the surprise provider of Pip's money later in the novel.

Mr. Jaggers...

...is a hot-shot lawyer. He's ruthless and intimidating but knows what's right and wrong.

Biddy...

...is Pip's childhood friend. She's plain but kind, and she always does the right thing.

Mr. Pumblechook...

...is Joe's uncle. He's obsessed with social status and money and he's quite boring.

Introduction

'Great Expectations' — Plot Summary

'Great Expectations'... what happens when?

You need to know *Great Expectations* almost as well as your own name. This little list of the main events will help you on your way, but it won't get you out of reading the book. There's no escaping that I'm afraid...

Chapters One to Ten — Pip wants to be a gentleman

- Pip is visiting his parents' graves when he's <u>attacked</u> by an <u>escaped</u> <u>convict</u>. The convict forces Pip to <u>steal</u> food and a metal file from his sister and brother-in-law.

- The next day Pip's just about to be <u>found out</u> when some <u>soldiers</u> arrive — they're looking for two convicts. Later they find them and <u>arrest</u> them. The convict that Pip already knows <u>lies</u> to protect him.

- Pip starts visiting <u>Miss Havisham</u>, a strange, rich old lady, so he can play with her daughter <u>Estella</u>. Estella's <u>cruel</u> to Pip. He <u>falls in love</u> with her anyway.

© Gerry Murray

Chapters Eleven to Nineteen — Pip's dream comes true

© ITV/Rex Features

- Miss Havisham talks to Pip's brother-in-law <u>Joe</u> about Pip becoming a <u>blacksmith</u>. She gives Joe some <u>money</u> to pay for the apprenticeship. Pip's <u>disappointed</u> — he'd hoped for <u>more</u>.

- Another convict <u>escapes</u> and Pip's sister is <u>attacked</u> with an old leg iron. Some of the characters think the attacker was the escaped <u>convict</u> but Pip and Joe think it was <u>Orlick</u>.

- Pip meets Mr Jaggers, who tells him he's been given a lot of <u>money</u> — but Jaggers can't say who it's from. Pip thinks it's from <u>Miss Havisham</u>. He moves to <u>London</u>.

Chapters Twenty to Thirty — Pip settles into his new life

- Pip meets <u>Herbert</u> — he's related to Miss Havisham and Pip once beat him in a <u>fight</u>. They become friends, and Herbert teaches Pip <u>manners</u>. He also explains that Miss Havisham was <u>jilted</u> and brought up Estella to get her <u>revenge</u> on men.

- <u>Joe</u> visits Pip in London. Pip's <u>ashamed</u> of him because he's not a <u>gentleman</u>. Joe tells Pip that Miss Havisham wants him to visit.

- Pip goes back to Kent and sees <u>Estella</u> again — he <u>loves</u> her more than ever. He doesn't <u>bother</u> to visit Joe.

© Keith Pattison

Chapters Thirty-One to Thirty-Nine — Pip meets the convict again

- Estella comes to live in London and Pip often visits — but he's jealous of her many admirers.

- Pip's sister dies. After her funeral, Pip promises Biddy that he'll come home more often — but she knows he won't.

- Herbert and Pip are in a lot of debt. Pip wants to help his friend, so he secretly pays a company to hire Herbert.

- Pip gets an odd visitor — Magwitch, the convict he helped. He's back from Australia where he's made his fortune. He tells Pip he's the one who made him a gentleman.

Chapters Forty to Forty-Nine — Estella breaks Pip's heart

- Magwitch stays with Pip in London, even though he'll be arrested and executed if he's caught in England. Herbert agrees to help Pip get Magwitch out of the country.

- Pip tells Estella he loves her. Estella says she's going to marry Bentley Drummle even though she doesn't love him. Miss Havisham has brought her up to never love anyone.

- Pip learns that Magwitch is in danger of being tracked down.

- Miss Havisham apologises to Pip for causing him to suffer the same way that she did. Her dress catches fire and Pip saves her, but she dies later.

Chapters Fifty to Fifty-Nine — Pip loses all his money

- Magwitch is caught trying to escape. He's sentenced to death but he's very ill and dies with Pip by his side. The court takes away all his money, so Pip is poor again.

- Pip gets ill. Joe looks after him and pays off all his debts. Pip plans to propose to Biddy, but she's already married Joe.

- Pip goes to Cairo to work with Herbert.

- Years later he meets Estella at Miss Havisham's house. Her husband's dead. It's not clear if Pip and Estella get together or not.

'Great Expectations' — the most Pip-ular book around...

So *Great Expectations* is basically a story about Pip growing up and realising what's important in life — convicts, blacksmiths and women called Estella... If you've got your head round the plot, move on to Section One. In your next revision break why not have a look at the *Great Expectations* cartoon at the back of the book...

Introduction

Life in the 1800s

The way people live in *Great Expectations* is a world away from today — no phones, no cars, no supermarkets... Knowing more about life in the 1800s should help you make more sense of the story.

Factories and cities were appearing for the first time

1) From <u>1780</u> people in Britain began to use coal-fired <u>steam engines</u> to run big <u>factories</u>. Many of these factories made <u>cloth</u>, which was sold all around the world.

> *Great Expectations* was <u>published</u> in <u>1860-61</u> but the story is <u>set</u> earlier, between about <u>1810 and 1840</u>. Dickens based the story and the settings on the <u>real world</u>, as he remembered it from his own <u>childhood</u>.

2) Before this, Britain used to be much more rural — <u>farming</u> was the most obvious way of making a living.

3) This period — where most people in Britain went from working in <u>farming</u> to working in <u>manufacturing</u> — was called the <u>Industrial Revolution</u>.

Life was as tough in the cities as it was in the countryside

1) Wages in the <u>countryside</u> were low, and <u>life was hard</u>. The population was <u>increasing</u> and there weren't enough jobs to go around.

2) By the early 1800s, hundreds of thousands of people had <u>moved</u> from farm jobs in the country to <u>factory jobs</u> in the <u>cities</u>. They <u>hoped</u> to find <u>better wages</u>, and better job security.

3) But factory workers often lived in cheap, <u>overcrowded housing</u>. Waste from the cities <u>polluted</u> rivers, and the air was thick with <u>fumes</u>. People easily became <u>ill</u> and people often <u>died young</u>.

© Illustrated London News Ltd/Mary Evans

Pip Moves From the Village to the City

*   Pip moves to London to <u>learn</u> how to be a <u>gentleman</u>. He thinks it will be full of <u>opportunities</u>.

*   In London the first things Pip notices are <u>filth</u>, <u>crime</u> and <u>squalor</u>. The city <u>corrupts</u> his natural kindness — he <u>ignores</u> his family and gets into <u>debt</u>.

*   He realises what's <u>important</u> in life on a trip to the <u>countryside</u>. He says, "when I... looked around a little more upon the outspread beauty, I felt that I was not nearly thankful enough".

*   But Dickens does not give an <u>unrealistic</u>, <u>idealised</u> view of the countryside either. Pip feels <u>restricted</u> and <u>unhappy</u> in the village. The marshes are <u>wild</u>, <u>isolated</u>, and sometimes <u>dangerous</u> — Pip is <u>threatened</u> twice in the marshes, first by Magwitch and later by Orlick.

Use context to understand the novel's settings...

All this stuff about dirty cities and factories sounds like History — hardly surprising given it all happened 200 years ago. You could write about how these problems were brand new for Dickens and his readers.

Crime

In the early 1800s there was a massive rise in crime rates, so dealing with crime and criminals was a hot topic. Not surprisingly Dickens included plenty of crime and criminals in *Great Expectations*.

Crime levels increased hugely during the 1800s

1) In <u>1800</u> there were about <u>5,000</u> crimes a year in Britain. By <u>1840</u> there were around <u>20,000</u> per year.

2) Many people were <u>forced</u> to <u>steal</u> because they had no work or money. Fear of prison was not as bad as fear of <u>starving to death</u>.

Prisons were becoming overcrowded

1) Because the number of crimes had risen so <u>quickly</u>, prisons became <u>overcrowded</u>. The government decided to use <u>old war ships</u> to hold some prisoners. They were known as '<u>hulks</u>' and some were moored on the river Thames and the river Medway.

> <u>Magwitch</u> and <u>Compeyson</u> escape from the hulks.

2) The hulks were often used to house prisoners who were due to be <u>transported</u> to British colonies abroad. In the early 1800s the authorities sent some <u>convicted criminals</u> (like Magwitch) to serve their <u>sentences</u> in <u>Australia</u>.

3) In Australia the prisoners had to do <u>tough manual labour</u>. Anyone who stepped out of line could be <u>whipped</u> or worse. Prisoners who behaved well were eventually <u>released</u> and could <u>earn a living</u> in Australia — but they were usually <u>not allowed</u> to return to Britain.

© Mary Evans Picture Library

Character — Magwitch

> After serving his sentence, Magwitch is <u>free</u> to make his <u>fortune</u> in Australia, which is how he earns the money he gives to Pip. But he is <u>sentenced to death</u> for coming back to England.

Prisons had changed by the time the novel was written

1) Dickens describes <u>prisons</u> and <u>attitudes to convicts</u> as they were at the <u>start of the century</u>. But the situation had <u>improved</u> by the time he was writing *Great Expectations*.

2) In the novel, Dickens uses Pip to voice his <u>own thoughts</u> about prisons in the early 1800s. Pip's experience presents the justice system as <u>unfair</u> and <u>ineffective</u>, and the prisons as <u>dirty</u> and <u>overcrowded</u>:

> • When Pip visits Newgate, he describes the <u>open courtyard</u> as an "ugly, disorderly, <u>depressing scene</u>".
>
> • Magwitch first committed crimes just to survive — he was an orphan with no one to care for him. He expected "to be <u>pitied</u>" by the <u>courts</u>, but they unfairly decided he was "<u>hardened</u>".
>
> • Pip can "scarcely believe..." that he saw "<u>two-and-thirty</u>" people being sentenced to <u>death</u> at once.

3) Dickens wrote many novels, articles and essays <u>criticising</u> the <u>justice system</u> in Victorian England. His writings raised <u>public awareness</u> of the problems, and helped <u>change</u> things for the <u>better</u>.

KEY QUOTE

"I was sent for life. It's death to come back."

Magwitch's transportation to Australia was a darn sight better than hanging, but it was still a very serious punishment. It meant never being able to return to England, and working incredibly hard for years.

Women and Children

Nowadays, in the UK at least, women can vote, go to university and work on the same terms as men. Children have rights to education and a safe home life. It was all very different in the 1800s...

Life was hard for children

1) <u>Attitudes to children</u> were completely different in the 1800s. Many people genuinely believed that children should be '<u>seen and not heard</u>' and that a <u>beating</u> was the best way to teach the difference between right and wrong. Children were supposed to be very <u>respectful</u> towards all adults.

2) Many children died in <u>childhood</u>. Pip having five <u>dead brothers</u> wasn't <u>unusual</u> for the time.

3) If a family was <u>short of money</u> the <u>children</u> were expected to go out to <u>work</u>. Some worked in <u>factories</u>. Others, like Pip, did <u>odd jobs</u> in the <u>fields</u>.

Historical Background

When he was <u>twelve</u>, Dickens himself had to give up his <u>education</u> and work in a <u>factory</u> for a while. He went back to school eventually, but <u>never forgot</u> his factory experience.

A decent education was too expensive for most people

Cartoon of a schoolroom, 1840.

© INTERFOTO / Sammlung Rauch / Mary Evans

1) There were no free schools, so about <u>half the population</u> never learned to <u>read and write</u> because they couldn't afford to go to school.

2) The standard of education on offer for most people was poor. Most local schools taught <u>basic reading</u>, <u>writing</u> and <u>maths</u> and not much else.

3) Some local schools were run by the <u>Church of England</u>. Others — like the one in Pip's village — were run by women in their own homes. These were called '<u>dame schools</u>'. Often <u>older pupils</u> like Biddy helped the teacher <u>run the school</u>.

Character — Pip

Pip is quick to see the <u>connection</u> between <u>education</u> and <u>social position</u>. That's why he's so keen to have <u>extra lessons</u> from Biddy.

4) Children from <u>rich families</u> usually had a much better education. They'd often have a <u>tutor</u> or governess who taught them <u>at home</u>. Some were sent to live with a <u>tutor</u>. For example, Pip is tutored by Mr Pocket.

Women were expected to take second place to men

Character — Estella

Estella's marriage to Drummle shows the <u>risks</u> for women in marriage. He gives her <u>wealth</u>, <u>security</u>, and <u>independence</u> from Miss Havisham. But he also <u>abuses</u> her, and she's very unhappy.

1) People believed a woman's place was <u>in the home</u>. Married women had <u>no legal rights</u>. All their property automatically went to their husbands.

2) But marriage was still <u>better</u> than being an '<u>old maid</u>'. There were few jobs for women, so marriage gave them some <u>financial security</u>. It also allowed women to become <u>independent</u> from their <u>family</u> and run their own home.

3) Dickens probably had quite <u>conventional views</u> about women's roles. The women shown as truly <u>lovable</u> in *Great Expectations* — Biddy, Clara, and Miss Skiffins — aren't wimps, but they are <u>quiet</u> and <u>well-behaved</u>.

Remember that education was different in the 1800s...

These days we're lucky to get free education and you don't get caned for forgetting your homework, but that's the way it was back then. If education pops up in your exam, you could use the info on this page.

Class and Social Rules

Here's a page about class... It's not because I'm obsessed with it, honest. But those Victorians really did have a class fixation. For more on this — you know you want it bad — see page 43.

To succeed in society you had to know the rules

1) <u>Class</u> was very <u>important</u> to people in the 1800s. Your class would determine what <u>kind of life</u> you had.

2) Having <u>good manners</u> helped to prove that you were part of <u>middle class 'society'</u>. <u>Table manners</u> were important because socialising often involved <u>meals</u>.

3) Middle and upper class people were also expected to use correct English, <u>without a regional accent</u>. Joe knows this, and <u>can't do it</u> — that's why he gets in such a <u>tangle</u> talking to Miss Havisham about Pip's apprenticeship.

© Illustrated London News Ltd/Mary Evans

4) During the Industrial Revolution it became easier for people to <u>get rich</u> by investing in <u>industry</u>. People who earned lots of money this way could <u>socialise</u> with the upper classes, but they were seen as '<u>lower</u>' or <u>less acceptable</u> than people who had <u>inherited</u> their wealth.

'Great Expectations' is about being a gentleman

Being a <u>gentleman</u> was considered a <u>good thing</u> — but what made someone a gentleman wasn't always <u>clear</u>:

- Being a 'gentleman' was often to do with a man's <u>social class</u> or <u>job</u>.

- <u>Upper class</u> men, <u>army officers</u> and <u>church ministers</u> might all be counted as gentlemen.

- Some people would say you could only be a gentleman if you <u>didn't need to work</u>. Others might say it was OK to work as long as you <u>didn't</u> work with your <u>hands</u>.

- There was also <u>another meaning</u> to the word 'gentleman' — having <u>strong morals</u> and being <u>kind</u>.

- Some people thought it <u>wasn't important</u> to be this kind of gentleman, because it didn't mean you'd become <u>rich</u> or accepted by the <u>upper classes</u>.

Dickens uses some characters to show that it's <u>better</u> to be a <u>kind</u>, <u>moral</u> gentleman than an <u>upper class</u> one:

1) Joe has some of the <u>qualities</u> of a gentleman — he <u>treats others well</u>, and has a strong sense of <u>right and wrong</u>. But some characters, like Pip, can't see Joe's gentlemanly nature because he works with his <u>hands</u>, and has <u>no social polish</u>. Others, like Miss Havisham, respect Joe's dignity and manners.

2) Bentley Drummle is <u>rich</u> and <u>upper class</u> so he's seen by society to be a gentleman. However, he's actually <u>rude</u>, <u>aggressive</u>, and <u>violent</u>. This shows that being a gentleman isn't necessarily a <u>good thing</u>.

> **Theme — Ambition**
>
> Pip and Magwitch both think being a gentleman is <u>desirable</u>, but have <u>no clear idea</u> of what a gentleman is.

"Yet a gentleman should not be unjust neither"

This stuff about being a gentleman keeps cropping up in the novel — it was a big deal for old Charlie. He wanted readers to think about what is and isn't important in life, and what being a decent chap is all about.

Practice Questions

Think of these ten practice questions like stepping stones. Step up to each one carefully and if you don't slip they'll take you safely across the flooded river. Page. River. This metaphor is confusing.

Quick Questions

1) What time period is *Great Expectations* set in?

2) Which of these best describes living conditions for poor people in cities in the 1800s:
   a) dirty and overcrowded   or   b) clean and spacious?

3) Why did the government have to use old war ships to imprison people, and what were the ships called?

4) Why was it so dangerous for Magwitch to come back to England?

5) Why was life for many children hard in the 1800s?

6) What was the name of the type of school Pip went to?

7) 'Estella marries Bentley Drummle in order to have more legal rights'. True or false?

8) Why were table manners important for members of the middle class?

9) How were middle class people supposed to speak?

10) How was a gentleman supposed to behave in the 1800s?

Analysis of Volume One: Chapters 1-3

This section talks about the whole novel, chapter by chapter. Use it to make sure you know the story inside-out, upside-down and left-to-right. If you just want a quick summary of the plot, have a look at p.4-5.

Pip is attacked by a convict

1) Pip's in the village <u>graveyard</u> reading his family's gravestones and trying to imagine what they look like. This introduces the reader to the idea that he's <u>searching for his true identity</u>.

2) Pip's <u>attacked</u> by a "fearful man". Dickens makes this scene more <u>dramatic</u> by using <u>shorter sentences</u>. Dickens also doesn't say who's speaking — this mimics Pip's <u>shock</u> and <u>confusion</u>.

3) The man is a <u>convict</u> who's escaped from a nearby prison ship. He orders Pip to bring him <u>food</u> ("wittles") and a <u>file</u> so he can get the <u>iron</u> off his leg. Pip's <u>afraid</u> so he obeys him.

Character — Pip

The novel starts with Pip by the <u>graves</u> of his <u>parents</u> and <u>brothers</u>. This makes the reader feel <u>sympathy</u> towards him.

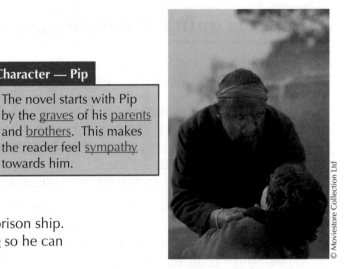

© Moviestore Collection Ltd

At home, Pip's in trouble with Mrs Joe

1) When Pip gets home he's <u>in trouble</u> with his sister, Mrs Joe. She has a "hard and heavy hand" and <u>beats</u> him with a stick called "<u>Tickler</u>". Pip's home life obviously isn't very <u>happy</u>.

Theme — Relationships

Pip's <u>friendship</u> with Joe <u>changes</u> when Pip gets rich — this is a really <u>important</u> part of the story.

2) Mrs Joe has <u>brought him up</u> since his parents died, but she's not really a <u>mother</u> to him — the fact that he calls her "<u>Mrs Joe</u>" instead of her <u>real name</u> shows that they're not <u>close</u>.

3) Dickens also introduces <u>Joe</u>, Pip's brother-in-law. Mrs Joe <u>beats</u> him too, and Pip sees him as an <u>equal</u> rather than as his <u>parent</u>.

KEY EVENT

Pip meets the convict again

1) On his way to meet the first man, Pip sees <u>another convict</u> in leg irons who tries to hit him, then disappears. This <u>mystery</u> helps to keep the reader <u>interested</u>.

2) When Pip hands over the <u>food</u> and <u>file</u> to the first convict, he starts off frightened, but then starts to <u>feel sorry</u> for the "awfully hungry" man. The convict calls him "<u>my boy</u>". They get on better this time — this hints at their <u>closer relationship</u> later on in the novel.

Writer's Techniques — Symbolism

When the convict is <u>eating</u>, Pip compares him to a <u>dog</u>, but not in a judgemental way. This <u>contrasts</u> with what he thinks about the way Magwitch <u>eats</u> in Chapter 40 (see p.22).

EXAM TIP

Talk about how Dickens creates sympathy for Pip...

Poor Pip. No treats for him on Christmas Eve — he only gets bread, tar water and an early night. Explain how Dickens squeezes as much sympathy as he can out of his readers — he wants them to be on Pip's side.

Analysis of Volume One: Chapters 4-6

Now Pip's delivered the food to the convict, he's just got to get through Christmas Day without Mrs Joe working out that he's been stealing bits of her Christmas dinner. Christmas just wasn't the same in those days.

Pip feels guilty about stealing from Mrs Joe

1) Pip <u>feels guilty</u> about helping the convict and <u>stealing</u> the <u>food</u> — he thinks he'll be <u>found out</u> at any moment.

2) But there is some <u>comedy</u> when Pumblechook drinks the brandy with the tar water in it. Pip describes his <u>reaction</u> as "an appalling spasmodic whooping-cough dance" — this <u>lightens</u> the <u>mood</u> of the chapter and makes Pumblechook seem even more <u>ridiculous</u>.

3) When Mrs Joe goes to find the pie Pip stole, he tries to <u>escape</u>, but he runs into some <u>soldiers</u> at the door carrying a "<u>pair of handcuffs</u>". Dickens finishes Chapter Four with a <u>cliffhanger</u> to keep his readers <u>interested</u>.

© AF archive / Alamy

Soldiers come looking for the convicts

1) At the beginning of Chapter Five, Dickens immediately <u>ends</u> the <u>suspense</u> he created at the end of the last chapter. The soldiers have come to <u>arrest</u> the two <u>convicts</u>, not Pip, and they need <u>Joe</u> to mend their <u>broken handcuffs</u>.

2) When the soldiers find the two <u>convicts</u>, they're <u>fighting</u> because they have a <u>grudge</u> against one another. The <u>relationship</u> between the two convicts is very important — it helps make Magwitch seem a more <u>realistic</u> character and creates a lot of <u>tension</u>.

Theme — Crime and Justice

Pip feels so <u>guilty</u> that he thinks he'll be <u>arrested</u> by a group of <u>soldiers</u> with "<u>muskets</u>". This isn't very <u>realistic</u>, and shows how <u>young</u> and immature Pip is. It also hints at how <u>involved</u> he'll be with <u>crime</u> for the rest of the novel.

Character — Magwitch

The convict <u>lies</u> to protect Pip. This is a <u>clue</u> that he's actually an <u>honourable</u> man.

3) Joe shows his <u>kindness</u> by saying even though he doesn't know what Magwitch's <u>crime</u> is, "we wouldn't have you <u>starved to death</u> for it".

4) The convict makes sure Pip won't get into <u>trouble</u> by saying he <u>stole</u> the food himself.

Pip gets away with his crimes, but he's not happy

1) Pip feels <u>torn</u>. He wants to <u>come clean</u> to Joe and tell him that he was the thief. But he's also <u>afraid</u> that if he does Joe will be <u>angry</u> and he'll <u>lose</u> the only <u>friend</u> he has.

2) In the end Pip decides to <u>say nothing</u>. It seems like a small thing at this point, but when Pip and Joe <u>grow apart</u> later in the story, this looks like the moment when things between them <u>begin to change</u>.

Write about the pace of the novel...

A lot's happened in just six chapters — Pip met the convict, they ate Christmas dinner, they chased two convicts over the marshes... You can comment on this fast-paced mix of drama and comedy. And gravy.

Analysis of Volume One: Chapters 7-10

After all the excitement of the opening chapters the next four chapters go at a steadier pace. Pip meets Miss Havisham and starts to dream of becoming a rich gentleman.

Pip meets Miss Havisham and Estella

KEY EVENT

1) Pip visits <u>Miss Havisham</u> for the first time. There are "<u>iron bars</u>" in the windows of her house, and the gate is always <u>locked</u>. This makes it seem like a <u>prison</u>.

2) Estella tells Pip his hands are "<u>coarse</u>", and he starts to feel <u>ashamed</u> of them. Pip's hands symbolise that he feels <u>unequal</u> to Estella, and when he <u>burns</u> his hands in Chapter 49, it's a sign that he's starting to <u>change</u>.

Writer's Techniques — Imagery

Dickens uses lots of <u>death-related imagery</u> to describe Miss Havisham. For example, Pip compares her to a "<u>skeleton</u> in the ashes of a rich dress". This gives the impression that her life is <u>already over</u> and she's waiting to <u>die</u>.

There's a lot about education in these chapters

1) Mr Wopsle's great-aunt's school is made to sound <u>ridiculous</u>. The students don't learn anything and Mr Wopsle's great-aunt spends most of her time in "a state of <u>coma</u>". Dickens is <u>satirising</u> (see p.52) the type of education many people would have received at the time.

Turning Point in the Action
After meeting Miss Havisham and Estella, Pip begins to feel unhappy about his social class and his future as a blacksmith.

Character — Joe

Joe tells Pip not to <u>worry</u> about what people like Miss Havisham and Estella think. Pip should <u>work hard</u> to make a living so he can "<u>live well</u> and <u>die happy</u>." He also tells him <u>not to lie</u> because "if you can't get to be oncommon through going straight, you'll never get it through going crooked." Although he isn't <u>educated</u>, some of Joe's advice is very <u>wise</u>.

2) However, Pip seems quite <u>keen</u> to be educated at this point — when Joe says "What a scholar you are", Pip says "I should like to be".

3) Once Pip meets Estella, he wants to be <u>better educated</u> so he can be her <u>equal</u>. He decides to take <u>extra lessons</u> from Biddy.

Joe and Pip meet a stranger at the pub

Writer's Techniques — Foreshadowing

Dickens <u>reminds</u> his readers about the <u>convict</u> because he wants to <u>foreshadow</u> Magwitch's return.

1) Joe and Pip meet a "<u>secret-looking man</u>" who uses a <u>file</u> to stir his drink. The man gives Pip some <u>money</u>.

2) The money and the file remind Pip of his <u>guilty feelings</u> about helping the convict escape — the money becomes a "<u>nightmare</u>" to him afterwards. This <u>foreshadows</u> the fact that <u>money</u> won't make Pip <u>happy</u>.

Foreshadowing is when a writer hints at something that happens later in the novel.

"The cold wind seemed to blow colder there"

Mrs Joe sees Pip's visit to Miss Havisham as a huge opportunity — she understands that the visit could make his "fortune". Her high expectations contrast with the cold, spooky atmosphere at Satis House.

Analysis of Volume One: Chapters 11-13

Pip meets two people in these chapters who will be really important in the rest of the story — Mr Jaggers and Herbert Pocket. The spiteful behaviour from Estella continues. Oh and Miss Havisham's still quite weird.

Pip goes back to Satis House

1) Miss Havisham's <u>relatives</u> visit her. She tells Pip they'll "<u>feast upon</u>" her when she dies. They're only after her <u>money</u> — they don't <u>care</u> about her. This is one of Dickens's <u>key messages</u> — money can <u>damage</u> the <u>relationships</u> between people.

2) Pip meets a "<u>pale young gentleman</u>" who challenges him to a <u>fight</u> which Pip wins.

3) Later he feels "<u>very uneasy</u>" about the fight and imagines that Miss Havisham will "draw a pistol" and <u>kill</u> him. This adds to the <u>guilt</u> he feels about helping the convict at the <u>beginning</u> of the novel.

© ITV/Rex Features

Pip's falling in love with Estella

Character — Miss Havisham

The way <u>Miss Havisham</u> says "Break their hearts my pride and hope, break their hearts and have no mercy" sounds like a <u>spell</u>. Pip seems to think she's quite spooky too — in the previous chapter he calls her "the <u>Witch</u> of the place" — but his opinion of her <u>changes</u> later on (see p.16).

1) Estella asks Pip "Am I <u>pretty</u>?" and "Am I <u>insulting</u>?" He <u>refuses</u> to answer her questions: "I shall not tell you".

2) The fact that he can't be <u>honest</u> about his feelings for Estella <u>foreshadows</u> how his life will be all about <u>appearances</u> once he's a gentleman.

3) Miss Havisham <u>encourages</u> Estella's cruel teasing. When Pip tells Miss Havisham that he thinks Estella is <u>pretty</u>, she listens "<u>greedily</u>" and she watches the <u>horrible</u> way Estella treats him with "<u>miserly relish</u>".

Joe visits Satis House

KEY EVENT

1) <u>Joe</u> is invited to Satis House to talk to Miss Havisham about Pip's <u>apprenticeship</u> as a blacksmith. He's so <u>shy</u> and <u>awkward</u> that he talks to Pip, not Miss Havisham. Pip's <u>ashamed</u> of his behaviour.

2) Pip thinks Miss Havisham will make him a <u>gentleman</u> by paying for his <u>education</u> and giving him some of her <u>money</u>. He's <u>disappointed</u> when she only gives Joe "five-and-twenty guineas" to cover the cost of his <u>apprenticeship</u>.

3) Being a <u>blacksmith</u> used to be Pip's <u>ambition</u>, but since meeting <u>Estella</u>, all he wants is to become a <u>gentleman</u>.

Writer's Techniques — Language

A lot of the words that Dickens uses to describe Pip's <u>apprenticeship</u> are also linked to <u>crime</u>. For example, Pip's taken to be "<u>bound</u>" to Joe and people look at him as if he's been caught "<u>red-handed</u>". This shows that Pip thinks training to be a blacksmith is like a <u>prison sentence</u>.

KEY QUOTE

"You are growing tall, Pip!"

These few chapters are where Pip stops being a little boy. He fights with Herbert, he gets a kiss from Estella and he signs up to be an apprentice, with Joe as his master — these are all signs that he's growing up.

Analysis of Volume One: Chapters 14-17

When Pip becomes Joe's apprentice, the regular visits to Satis House stop. Pip doesn't stop thinking about Estella though, and he keeps on moping about her all the way through the book, so you'd better get used to it.

Pip starts work at the forge

1) Pip's now <u>working for Joe</u> and feels <u>unhappy</u> about his <u>work</u> and <u>background</u>, even though he knows he shouldn't — "It is a most miserable thing to feel <u>ashamed of home</u>."

2) When Pip's been Joe's apprentice for a <u>year</u> he asks him for a half-day off to visit Miss Havisham — but really it's <u>Estella</u> he wants to see.

3) When Orlick gets <u>annoyed</u> about this, he insults Mrs Joe and Joe's forced to fight him to <u>defend</u> his wife. Mrs Joe gets very <u>excited</u> by the fight — she has a "fit of clappings and screamings". The fact she seems to <u>enjoy</u> it is <u>similar</u> to the way <u>Estella</u> seems to enjoy Pip's fight with the "pale young gentleman".

4) When Pip gets to <u>Satis House</u>, he finds that Estella has gone abroad, "educating for a lady". Miss Havisham seems <u>delighted</u> that Pip's disappointed. She <u>rubs it in</u> by saying she's "far out of reach... admired by all".

© ITV/Rex Features

Mrs Joe is attacked

1) On the way home, Pip hears cannons firing from the <u>prison ships</u> — the signal that a convict's escaped. Dickens is hinting that <u>danger</u> might be coming.

2) Mrs Joe is <u>attacked</u> — almost everyone assumes the attacker is a convict because the <u>weapon</u> was a convict's leg iron, filed off a long time ago.

3) Pip realises it's "my convict's iron" and feels <u>responsible</u> for the attack. It's another <u>symbol</u> of how crime surrounds Pip throughout the novel (see p.46).

> **Character — Pip**
>
> Pip starts to call Mrs Joe "<u>my sister</u>". He feels <u>pity</u> for her after the attack.

Biddy comes to live at the forge

> **Character — Pip**
>
> Pip realises that Biddy is "<u>immeasurably better</u> than Estella" but he can't <u>make himself</u> love her. He actually tells Biddy this, which seems pretty <u>harsh</u>.

1) Mrs Joe is left <u>brain-damaged</u> and can't look after herself so <u>Biddy</u> comes to live at the forge to help.

2) Pip tells her about his <u>ambitions</u> to be a <u>gentleman</u> and she asks whether he wouldn't be "<u>happier</u> as you are?" This is a key <u>message</u> in *Great Expectations* — <u>money</u> and <u>social position</u> don't necessarily lead to <u>happiness</u>.

Write about how violence is common in the novel...

You can impress the examiner by writing about how violence in the novel isn't just limited to out-and-out criminals and bad eggs — it's so widespread that even the usually-gentle Joe gets into a fight. Yikes.

Analysis of Volume One: Chapters 18-19

Pip should be happy at this point, with nice Joe and Biddy to look after him and a steady job. But he's not happy — he still wants to be a gentleman and impress Estella. Luckily for Pip things are about to change...

Pip learns that he has great expectations

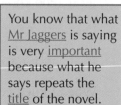

1) Pip finds out he's got "great expectations". He's <u>thrilled</u> — it's just what he always <u>dreamed of</u>. He thinks <u>Miss Havisham</u> has given him the money — Mr Jaggers is her <u>lawyer</u>, and her <u>relative</u> will be Pip's tutor.

© ITV/Rex Features

2) Mr Jaggers says he's <u>only</u> helping Pip because he's being <u>paid</u> — "I am paid for my services, or I shouldn't render them."

3) Joe is the <u>opposite</u> of this. He <u>refuses</u> to take any money for <u>losing Pip</u> as his apprentice — "Lord forbid that I should want anything for not standing in Pip's way".

> You know that what <u>Mr Jaggers</u> is saying is very <u>important</u> because what he says repeats the <u>title</u> of the novel.

> **Turning Point in the Action**
> Pip finds out that his dream of being a gentleman is going to come true.

Pip starts to look down on Joe and Biddy

1) Pip starts to treat Joe and Biddy <u>badly</u>. He's <u>embarrassed</u> by Joe and tells Biddy he wishes Joe had <u>posher manners</u>. He gets annoyed with Biddy for no reason, and then <u>forgives</u> her "<u>Handsomely</u>" — he's starting to become quite <u>obnoxious</u>.

2) That night, Pip thinks it's <u>strange</u> that "this first night of my bright fortunes should be the <u>loneliest</u> I had ever known." His great expectations are <u>taking him away</u> from the people who <u>love</u> him — this is a sign that he won't be <u>happy</u> in his new life.

Pip prepares to move to London

1) Pip goes to town to order some <u>new clothes</u>. Everyone treats him in a <u>respectful</u> and <u>friendly</u> way when they hear about his new <u>money</u> — they're just <u>pretending</u> to like him now he's rich. This <u>contrasts</u> with the way that Joe and Biddy treat him — as if <u>nothing's happened</u>.

> **Theme — Social Class**
> Dickens <u>ridicules</u> the way people <u>pretend</u> to like Pip by saying that even the <u>cows</u> on the marshes "wear a more <u>respectful</u> air" now that he's <u>rich</u>.

2) Pip's <u>opinion</u> of Miss Havisham <u>changes</u> as soon as he thinks she's given him <u>money</u> — instead of a <u>witch</u>, he now sees her as his "<u>fairy godmother</u>".

3) At the end of <u>Volume One</u>, Pip seems <u>torn</u>. The <u>mists</u> rise and Pip says "the <u>world</u> lay <u>spread before me</u>." This image makes him seem <u>optimistic</u> about his future, but part of him also wants to go back to the <u>forge</u> — he talks a lot about his "<u>deliberations</u>".

EXAM TIP
Talk about the structure of the novel...

Volume One covers Pip's early life, and ends as he's leaving to become a fancy gentleman. You could write about how Dickens uses the structure of the novel to mark the different stages in Pip's life (see p.52).

Analysis of Volume Two: Chapters 20-22

Volume Two starts with Pip's arrival in London — it's a new phase in his life and the story. Pip still isn't super-confident in these chapters, but he's definitely a world away from the snivelling boy in the graveyard.

Pip arrives in London

Writer's Techniques

Dickens uses <u>language</u> such as "<u>gloomy</u>", "<u>moth-eaten</u>" and "<u>weather-stained</u>" right at the beginning of Chapter 20 to <u>emphasise</u> how horrible Pip finds London.

1) When Pip <u>arrives</u> in London he finds it "rather ugly, crooked, narrow and dirty". He sees the <u>blood and filth</u> of Smithfield meat market and the <u>gallows</u> at Newgate Prison — "This was horrible, and gave me a sickening idea of London".

2) It's not just London which is <u>unpleasant</u>. Mr Jaggers, the lawyer in charge of Pip's fortune, isn't nice either. He <u>threatens</u> his clients and they're "<u>terrified</u>" of him. For more on Jaggers, see p.38.

3) Pip's going to stay with <u>Herbert</u>, his tutor's son, for the weekend . His flat is in <u>Barnard's Inn</u> — not a smart <u>hotel</u> owned by someone called Barnard, as Pip imagines, but a <u>run-down</u> apartment building. Barnard's Inn is one of many things in London which isn't how Pip <u>expects</u> it will be.

Pip and Herbert are soon friends

1) As soon as Herbert arrives they <u>recognise</u> each other — they once had a <u>fight</u> at Miss Havisham's house (see p.14). Then the chapter <u>ends</u> — the reader has to <u>wait</u> to find out whether they <u>fight</u> again.

Theme — Social Class

The nicknames "prowling <u>boy</u>" and "pale young <u>gentleman</u>" that Herbert and Pip gave each other after the fight showed that they were from different <u>social classes</u>. Now that Pip has expectations, he and Herbert are <u>equals</u>.

© Moviestore Collection Ltd

2) The two boys <u>laugh</u> about their fight and have <u>dinner</u>. Pip asks Herbert to <u>correct</u> his <u>table manners</u> — he understands that eating politely is part of being a <u>gentleman</u>.

Herbert tells Pip about Miss Havisham

1) Miss Havisham's <u>half-brother</u> and one of his <u>friends</u> betrayed her to get hold of her <u>fortune</u>. She was <u>abandoned</u> by her lover on her <u>wedding day</u>. This <u>finally</u> explains why she's so <u>weird</u>.

2) Herbert says that she <u>adopted</u> Estella and raised her to "wreak <u>revenge</u> on all the male sex". We find out more about this in Chapter 38.

Character — Pip

Pip's too <u>blinded</u> by his feelings for Estella to pay any <u>attention</u> to what Herbert <u>says</u> about her.

3) Herbert's father, Matthew Pocket, tried to <u>warn</u> Miss Havisham that she was being <u>tricked</u>. Pip realises that Matthew <u>isn't</u> after Miss Havisham's <u>money</u> like the rest of her <u>relatives</u>.

 KEY QUOTE

"all asmear with filth and fat and blood and foam"

London is less fun than Pip expects. It's dirty, confusing and full of nasty criminals. Even his flat is a disappointment. The only really good thing about Pip's first day is meeting Herbert — he's a decent chap.

Analysis of Volume Two: Chapters 23-27

These chapters describe Pip's life during his first weeks in London. Not much happens but you do find out more about some important characters, like Wemmick, Jaggers and the odious Drummle.

Pip is staying with the Pockets

1) Pip stays with Herbert's father, Matthew Pocket, who's going to be his tutor. Matthew introduces Pip to the other boys studying with him — Startop and Bentley Drummle. You'll see more of them later.

2) Drummle and Mrs Pocket have a long, snobby conversation about titles and family history. They both think they should belong to a higher class and aren't happy with their lives. Pip criticises them for this — he can't see that this is just the same as him not wanting to be a blacksmith.

> **Theme — Social Class**
>
> Dickens uses Mrs Pocket to ridicule the class system. She thinks she has noble ancestors, but she has no idea how to do anything practical — she's "perfectly helpless and useless."

Pip gets to know his new friends

1) A few weeks after he arrives in London, Pip goes to Wemmick's house for dinner. It's the nicest place Pip visits but Wemmick isn't rich, or a gentleman. He bought his house "a bit at a time" which contrasts with Pip getting rich suddenly. Dickens is showing that happiness doesn't always come from money or class.

2) But Wemmick's house is like a castle — it has "fortifications" and a drawbridge so Wemmick can "cut off the communication" — this suggests that the world outside Wemmick's home is dangerous.

3) Soon afterwards, Pip, Herbert, Drummle and Startop go to Jaggers's house for a dinner party. Jaggers makes a strange show of his housekeeper Molly's strong wrists. They're badly scarred.

> Molly becomes important later in the story (see p.25).

4) Jaggers is fascinated by Drummle, but tells Pip to "Keep as clear of him as you can." This foreshadows the fact that Drummle will cause trouble for Pip in the future.

Joe comes to London

© Moviestore Collection Ltd

1) Biddy writes to Pip saying Joe's coming to London. Pip's so ashamed of Joe that he wants to keep him away from people he knows in London, even if it means "paying money" — he thinks that everything in life can be bought.

2) Joe feels awkward in the city — he can't stop fiddling with his hat and he calls Pip "sir". He's also upset that Pip doesn't have time for him anymore, though he's much too polite to say this out loud.

3) Pip feels guilty that he was distant and cold with Joe. He follows him onto the street but Joe's already gone.

EXAM TIP

Mention how symbolism is used in the novel...

If you talk about symbols in the exam, you need to explain what they mean. Wemmick's castle is a symbol of the danger of the outside world. It also shows how good things come to those who don't flash their cash.

Analysis of Volume Two: Chapters 28-31

About six pages ago, the two one-pound notes left by the stranger at the Three Jolly Bargemen seemed like an absolute fortune, but now Pip's spending his cash hand over fist. He's changing fast in his new life...

Pip goes to Kent

1) Pip goes to Kent to see Miss Havisham and Estella. There are two <u>convicts</u> on the coach and one is the man who gave Pip <u>two one-pound notes</u> in Chapter Ten.

> **Theme — Violence and Punishment**
>
> Pip's <u>constantly</u> surrounded by <u>crime</u> — this hints at where his <u>money's</u> really from.

2) Pip's <u>certain</u> that Miss Havisham wants him to marry Estella — "it <u>could not fail</u> to be her intention to bring us together." He even compares himself to a "<u>Knight</u> of romance". This shows how caught up in his <u>dream</u> he is.

3) When he sees Estella, she <u>warns</u> Pip that she has "<u>no heart</u>". This suggests that she doesn't want to <u>hurt</u> Pip as much as Miss Havisham would like her to.

4) Miss Havisham commands Pip to <u>love Estella</u> — "Love her, love her, love her!" — like a <u>spell</u>. That night, Pip repeats — "I love her, I love her, I love her!" He's being <u>manipulated</u> by Miss Havisham.

© ITV/Rex Features

> Pip's <u>surprised</u> that <u>Orlick's</u> working as a gatekeeper at Miss Havisham's. He tells Jaggers he doesn't think he's <u>right</u> for the job so Jaggers has him <u>fired</u>. This is <u>important</u> later on (see p.25).

Pip returns to London without visiting Joe

KEY EVENT

1) When Pip leaves London to go to Kent he's still <u>feeling bad</u> about the way he treated <u>Joe</u> when he came to London. He says it's "<u>clear</u> that I must stay at Joe's." But later on that day he starts to "invent reasons and make excuses" for staying somewhere else.

2) When Estella says Pip's old friends are "<u>unfit company</u>" for him now he's a gentleman, he makes up his mind <u>not</u> to visit Joe. He only cares about <u>Estella's opinion</u>, not about <u>Joe's feelings</u>.

3) Pip sends Joe "a <u>penitential</u> codfish and barrel of oysters" because he feels guilty for not visiting him. He doesn't realise that Joe doesn't want <u>money</u>, or gifts — he just wants Pip's <u>friendship</u>. The fact that Pip is starting to <u>regret</u> his behaviour shows that he's not entirely <u>selfish</u>.

Pip and Herbert see a play

1) Pip and Herbert go to see <u>Mr Wopsle</u> (who's calling himself "Mr Waldengarver" to sound more <u>respectable</u>) in a performance of Hamlet. The play is a <u>disaster</u> and Mr Wopsle is a laughing-stock. Dickens suggests that people shouldn't <u>pretend</u> to be something they're <u>not</u>.

2) The <u>disastrous</u> performance is also a nice <u>break</u> from all the <u>heartache</u> and misery of the last chapters.

KEY QUOTE

"if I adored her before, I now doubly adore her."

These chapters show how much Pip has changed since he was a boy. He thinks of himself as a gentleman and lives in a different world to Joe. The only thing that's stayed the same is the way he feels about Estella.

Analysis of Volume Two: Chapters 32-35

This summary is about three hundred and fifty pages shorter than the actual book. Even so there's a teeny weeny chance your spirits are flagging... so you might like to know you're over halfway through. Chin up.

Wemmick gives Pip a tour of Newgate Prison

1) Pip goes to collect Estella when she <u>arrives</u> in London. While he's waiting <u>Wemmick</u> shows him around <u>Newgate prison</u>.

2) Afterwards, Pip feels as if the air of the <u>prison</u> is still <u>clinging</u> to him — he's <u>contaminated</u> by a "taint of prison and crime". He thinks it's <u>strange</u> that crime still <u>stains</u> his "fortune and advancement." This is <u>ironic</u> because soon he'll realise just how <u>much</u> his expectations rely on <u>crime</u> (see p.21).

©TopFoto.co.uk

> ### Historical Background — Crime
>
> Dickens probably includes such a <u>long description</u> of the <u>prison</u> because he was very interested in <u>prison reform</u> and changes to the <u>justice system</u>.

Pip's confused about his feelings for Estella

1) Pip takes Estella to a house in <u>Richmond</u> where she's going to be staying. She's <u>more polite</u> to Pip than ever before and even <u>flirts</u> with him a bit. She uses his <u>name</u> for the first time instead of calling him "<u>boy</u>". Pip knows she's <u>manipulating him</u> to make him love her.

2) He looks at Estella's new home, and says "I never was happy with her, but always miserable." He's beginning to realise that his ambition of marrying Estella would only have ended <u>badly</u>. This shows that he's starting to <u>mature</u> as a character.

> ### Character — Estella
>
> Estella feels as if she and Pip are being controlled by <u>Miss Havisham</u> — she says they are "mere <u>puppets</u>".

KEY EVENT

Pip begins to realise he's behaving badly

1) Pip starts to feel <u>guilty</u> about his bad behaviour. He hasn't been to see <u>Joe and Biddy</u>. He's been wasting money and getting into <u>debt</u> and he's got <u>Herbert</u> into debt too.

2) <u>Mrs Joe dies</u> and Pip goes to her funeral. At the funeral, the guests get their handkerchiefs out because they're <u>told to</u>, not because they feel <u>sad</u>. Again, <u>appearances</u> are more important than <u>reality</u>.

3) Afterwards, Pip has a talk with Biddy. He says he'll <u>visit more often</u> now Joe is alone, but Biddy doesn't believe him. Pip's offended but also knows that Biddy is <u>right to doubt him</u>.

> ### Theme — Relationships
>
> Biddy is the only person who's completely <u>honest</u> with Pip, but he just gets <u>angry</u> with her. He can't <u>accept</u> that what she says is <u>true</u>.

EXAM TIP

Write about how Dickens makes Pip a flawed character...

A prison trip, a coach ride and a funeral... If you're thinking these few chapters aren't exactly gripping, that's fair enough. The important thing to say is that this is where Pip starts to realise he's not Mr Wonderful.

Analysis of Volume Two: Chapters 36-39

Pip's a fool. He ignores the one man who's always been kind to him (Joe) and obsesses over a woman who couldn't care less about him (Estella). But in Chapter 37 he does do something good for a change...

Pip has his 21st birthday

1) On his <u>21st birthday</u> Pip hopes to find out <u>who</u> gave him all his <u>money</u> but Jaggers still can't tell him.

2) Pip decides to use some of the <u>£500</u> he gets for his birthday to secretly <u>help Herbert</u> get a job. He feels <u>responsible</u> for getting Herbert into debt and <u>guilty</u> because he thinks he ruined Herbert's chances of <u>inheriting money</u> from Miss Havisham.

3) Wemmick <u>agrees to help</u> Pip. They arrange for Herbert to join a young merchant called Clarriker in his new <u>shipping firm</u>.

Theme — Relationships

This is one of the only <u>nice</u> things Pip does. The fact that Pip keeps it a <u>secret</u> shows that he's genuinely trying to <u>help</u> Herbert rather than <u>show off</u> his generosity. It shows how <u>strong</u> his <u>friendship</u> with Herbert is.

Pip can't get Estella out of his head

1) Estella has lots of <u>admirers</u> and it's "<u>torture</u>" for Pip to see her with them — but he can't help loving her. Estella tells Pip she <u>doesn't love him</u> because she has <u>no feelings</u> for anyone.

2) Estella <u>does</u> seem to think about Pip in a <u>different way</u> to her admirers — she tells him that she deceives and entraps "all of them <u>but you</u>."

3) Pip and Estella go to visit <u>Miss Havisham</u>. Miss Havisham accuses Estella of having a <u>cold heart</u>. Estella replies that she is exactly as Miss Havisham <u>trained her</u> to be — "I am what you have <u>made</u> me." This makes the reader <u>change</u> their opinion of Miss Havisham — they start to feel <u>sorry</u> for her.

Pip's convict makes a dramatic return

KEY EVENT

Turning Point in the Action
Pip finally finds out who his money is from.

1) When Pip's twenty-three the <u>convict</u> Pip helped as a boy visits him. It turns out that <u>he's</u> the one who gave Pip the <u>money</u>. He's made a fortune in Australia and <u>Pip</u> has been living on this fortune all these years.

2) Pip is <u>horrified</u> — his money's nothing to do with Miss Havisham so she can't want him to marry Estella. He realises all his theories about his "great expectations" were "<u>a mere dream</u>".

3) Magwitch is only interested in Pip's <u>appearance</u> and his <u>possessions</u> — he admires Pip's <u>watch</u>, <u>ring</u> and <u>clothes</u>. He thinks it's <u>material</u> things like this which make Pip a <u>gentleman</u>.

Character — Magwitch

Magwitch sees <u>Pip</u> like a <u>possession</u> at this point — he says he's "the <u>owner</u>" of a gentleman. This <u>contrasts</u> with Chapter 54, when he seems to just enjoy <u>spending time</u> with Pip.

"I began fully to know how wrecked I was"

Volume Two started with Pip leaving to live in London, in a fairly hopeful frame of mind. When Volume Two ends, Pip is sheltering a wanted man, and his dreams of marrying Estella are shattered. Poor Pip.

Analysis of Volume Three: Chapters 40-42

So, here we are at the beginning of Volume Three. In the first three chapters, Pip learns more about what Magwitch has been up to in the fourteen years since he first reared his less-than-pretty head on the marshes.

Magwitch and Pip get to know each other

1) At the <u>very start</u> of Volume Three Pip realises that someone might be <u>following</u> Magwitch. This gives the volume a <u>tense</u> atmosphere.

2) The convict eats in a <u>rough</u>, <u>greedy</u> way that reminds Pip of a dog. Pip's <u>disgusted</u> by Magwitch — even in respectable clothes Pip feels he still looks like "the <u>slouching fugitive</u> on the marshes."

3) Basically, Pip's <u>horrified</u> by the whole situation. He calls Magwitch "my <u>terrible</u> patron" and goes to Jaggers to check the story's <u>true</u>. He desperately wants it to be a <u>lie</u> so he'll still have a chance of marrying <u>Estella</u>.

Writer's Techniques — Symbolism

The <u>image</u> of Magwitch as a <u>dog</u> is the <u>same</u> as the one in Chapter Three but this time Pip thinks he's "uncouth, noisy, and greedy." Now he's <u>rich</u>, he looks down on Magwitch's <u>animal-like</u> behaviour.

Herbert helps Pip make an escape plan

Theme — Relationships

Herbert "received" Pip "with <u>open arms</u>" after finding out about Magwitch. This shows that he's a <u>true friend</u> to Pip.

1) Herbert's just as keen as Pip to <u>get rid</u> of Magwitch. Pip doesn't want <u>anything</u> more to do with Magwitch and tells Herbert he'll <u>refuse</u> to take any more of his <u>money</u>.

2) Pip's <u>worried</u> that Magwitch will turn himself in to the <u>police</u> if Pip refuses his money. Pip knows he'd feel really <u>guilty</u> if Magwitch was <u>arrested</u> so they decide to get Magwitch <u>out of the country</u> to stop him.

Pip feels sorry for Magwitch

1) Magwitch grew up <u>homeless</u> and with <u>no parents</u>. He lived by "Tramping, begging, thieving, working sometimes when I could..."

Context — The Poor

Dickens had a lot of <u>sympathy</u> for <u>poor children</u>. He suggests that Magwitch <u>had to</u> steal because he was <u>starving</u> — "I must put something into my stomach, mustn't I?"

2) As an adult he committed some <u>crimes</u> with a man called Compeyson, and was sent to <u>prison</u> several times.

3) As Pip listens to the story, he feels "<u>great pity</u>" for Magwitch instead of being <u>disgusted</u> by him. Pip's <u>slowly learning</u> that Magwitch isn't such a <u>bad</u> man but he's not convinced yet.

Theme — Social Class

Magwitch got a much <u>harsher sentence</u> than Compeyson because Compeyson was educated and looked like a <u>gentleman</u>.

© ITV/Rex Features

EXAM TIP

Mention that Pip begins to feel sorry for Magwitch...

Show the examiner that you understand how characters develop. For most of the book Pip is a daydreamer, but in Volume Three he finally starts to get a grip — which is reflected in his changing opinion of Magwitch.

Analysis of Volume Three: Chapters 43-46

Pip doesn't know how long he's going to be out of the country with Magwitch, so he decides to visit Satis House before he goes. He meets Drummle again and has a good old moan at Estella and Miss Havisham.

Pip meets Drummle and acts like a snob

1) On his way to Satis House, Pip meets <u>Bentley Drummle</u>. Pip <u>copies</u> everything Drummle does — for example, Drummle <u>pushes</u> Pip and Pip pushes him back. Pip's <u>acting</u> like Drummle because Drummle's a <u>gentleman</u>, but he just ends up looking <u>childish</u>.

2) When Pip says that even when he loses his <u>temper</u>, he doesn't <u>throw glasses</u>, Drummle replies, "<u>I do</u>". This shows that even people from the <u>higher classes</u> don't always <u>behave</u> very well.

Pip confronts Miss Havisham and Estella

1) Miss Havisham admits that she <u>used Pip</u> to get at her <u>greedy relatives</u>. It's the <u>first sign</u> that she feels <u>guilty</u> about what she's done to Pip.

2) Pip tells Miss Havisham that Herbert and Matthew Pocket <u>deserve more</u> from her. Apart from getting Herbert a <u>job</u>, it's one of the only <u>unselfish</u> things Pip does in the novel.

3) When Pip tells Estella how he feels, Dickens <u>emphasises</u> her inability to feel emotion by <u>repeating</u> three times that she's "<u>unmoved</u>".

4) She says she <u>can't</u> feel love for anyone, but Pip is the <u>only</u> person she would <u>admit</u> this to. Her <u>honesty</u> suggests that her relationship with Pip is <u>special</u> to her in some way.

Theme — Relationships

Estella thinks that by <u>marrying Drummle</u> she'll be <u>free</u> from Miss Havisham's control — deciding to marry him was her "<u>own act</u>", not Miss Havisham's. But by <u>not</u> marrying for <u>love</u> she's actually doing what Miss Havisham <u>wanted</u> her to do all along.

5) Chapter 44 ends on a <u>cliffhanger</u> — Pip's given a <u>note</u> from Wemmick saying — "<u>DON'T GO HOME</u>."

Photo: akg-images / album / Rank

Pip and Magwitch are being watched

1) Pip sleeps in a <u>hotel</u> for the night. The <u>description</u> of the hotel is fairly <u>comic</u> — Pip describes the bed as "a despotic monster" and spends most of the night worrying that insects will fall on him. This <u>lightheartedness</u> makes these chapters a little <u>less intense</u>.

Writer's Techniques

The <u>danger</u> Magwitch is in gives the story a <u>tense atmosphere</u>.

2) Pip goes to see Magwitch and finds him "<u>softened</u>" — Magwitch himself <u>hasn't changed</u>, but Pip <u>feels</u> softer towards him now. He's become <u>nicer</u> now that all his dreams have gone.

KEY QUOTE

"I am as unhappy as you can ever have meant me to be."

Meek, mild-mannered little Pip starts to get a few things off his chest in Chapter 44. He doesn't actually lose his rag, but it's the first time you see him properly stand up to Miss Havisham for manipulating him.

Analysis of Volume Three: Chapters 47-49

Dare I say it... Yes, I'll admit it — I think this is actually starting to get exciting. All that stuff about Estella and the money is left to one side for a bit and in the next few chapters the story turns into more of a thriller.

Pip is followed by Compeyson

1) Pip still thinks about Estella, but his "dominant anxiety" is now Magwitch and getting him out of the country safely. This shows that Pip is becoming more selfless.

2) Pip goes to see Mr Wopsle in another play. Wopsle tells him that Compeyson was sitting behind Pip in the theatre, but he disappeared at the end of the performance. Wopsle says he was sitting "like a ghost." This makes Compeyson seem very scary but it also foreshadows his death.

Pip learns about Estella's family

1) Pip meets Jaggers's housekeeper, Molly, again. Her eyes and the way she moves her fingers remind Pip of Estella. By the time dinner's over he's convinced that she's Estella's mother.

2) It's ironic that the similarity between Molly's "disfigured" and "scarred" wrists and Estella's fine hands are what makes him realise they're related.

Pip makes peace with Miss Havisham

KEY EVENT

Character — Pip

Pip doesn't ask for anything for himself from Miss Havisham — this shows how much he's grown as a character.

1) Miss Havisham begs Pip for forgiveness. She agrees to pay the rest of the money to Clarriker's for Herbert — she's not just saying sorry, she's also showing how sorry she is. Dickens is encouraging the reader to feel sympathy for Miss Havisham here.

2) Miss Havisham's intentions haven't always been bad — when she adopted Estella she wanted to "save her from misery like my own" but now she realises that she "stole her heart away, and put ice in its place."

Writer's Techniques — Imagery

Dickens often uses really cold images to describe Estella — they match the coldness of her personality.

© Nigel Norrington/ArenaPAL

3) When Pip leaves Satis House he has a vision of Miss Havisham hanging from a beam. He's worried, so he goes back and finds Miss Havisham with her dress on fire. He puts out the flames with a tablecloth — finally destroying the rotting wedding feast. This symbolises that Miss Havisham is finally freed from her obsession.

4) Pip's hands are badly burnt. This shows that he's becoming less selfish — he cares more about Miss Havisham's safety than his own. It's as if the fire has burnt away all of his snobbery and arrogance and he can finally become a better person.

KEY QUOTE

"Assistance was sent for and I held her until it came"

The fire at Miss Havisham's signifies the end of lots of things — the end of her obsession with her failed wedding, the end of her power over Pip, and the end of Pip's selfishness. Big changes are afoot...

Analysis of Volume Three: Chapters 50-53

Uh-oh... Pip's burns are a bit of a spanner in the works for the escape attempt — hands are handy for rowing. Luckily Herbert has a back-up plan. But as soon as this problem is dealt with a new one rears its ugly head...

Pip realises that Magwitch is Estella's father

1) Herbert tells Pip more about Magwitch's past. When Magwitch was living rough he had a <u>child</u> with a homeless woman. She was accused of <u>murdering</u> somebody soon afterwards. Pip realises that the woman was <u>Molly</u> and the little girl was <u>Estella</u>.

Writer's Techniques

When Dickens finally reveals the <u>truth</u> about Magwitch all the strands of the novel finally come <u>together</u>.

Theme — Social Class

It's <u>ironic</u> that Pip wanted to be a <u>gentleman</u> to impress <u>Estella</u> — she's even lower class than him because she's the daughter of two <u>criminals</u>.

2) Herbert also says that Magwitch felt "<u>pity</u>" and "<u>forbearance</u>" towards the mother, and he "<u>grieved</u>" for the <u>child</u> he lost. This is another clue that he's a <u>good</u> and <u>honourable</u> man.

3) Jaggers eventually admits that <u>Molly</u> had a <u>little girl</u> at the time of her <u>trial</u> for murder. He gave the child to Miss Havisham to <u>save</u> it from a life of <u>crime</u> and <u>misery</u>.

Pip and Herbert plan the escape

1) Pip's arms and hands are slowly <u>recovering</u>, but they're "<u>disfigured</u>". These scars are a permanent <u>reminder</u> of his bad behaviour and the fact that he's <u>moved on</u> from it.

2) Wemmick sends a note to say it's <u>time</u> to get Magwitch <u>out of London</u>. He tells Pip to <u>burn</u> it after he's read it — this adds to the atmosphere of <u>secrecy</u> and <u>danger</u>.

© Gerry Murray

Theme — Relationships

At an inn Pip hears how Pumblechook is still <u>taking the credit</u> for his good fortune. For the first time in ages he thinks about <u>Biddy</u> and <u>Joe</u> who have never asked him for <u>anything</u>.

3) Pip gets a <u>mysterious note</u> telling him to go to a sluice-house on the <u>marshes</u> in Kent. He's so <u>worried</u> about something happening to Magwitch that he decides to go. He really <u>cares</u> about what happens to Magwitch now.

Orlick attacks Pip

1) On his way to the sluice-house the <u>sky</u> is full of a "<u>red</u> large moon" and there's a "<u>melancholy wind</u>" on the marshes. Nature seems threatening — this gives the chapter a <u>scary atmosphere</u> and suggests that <u>something bad's</u> going to happen.

2) When he arrives, Pip is attacked and <u>tied up</u> by <u>Orlick</u>. Orlick feels as if Pip's always getting <u>in his way</u> — he got him <u>fired</u> from Miss Havisham's and he thinks Pip gave him a "bad name" to <u>Biddy</u>.

3) When he thinks he's <u>going to die</u>, Pip realises what's really <u>important</u> — he feels <u>guilty</u> about his past and is <u>sad</u> that no one would know "how <u>sorry</u> I had been that night". He's finally <u>growing up</u>.

4) Luckily for Pip, <u>Herbert</u> arrives just in the nick of time to <u>save</u> him.

EXAM TIP

Write about Herbert's importance in the story...

What would Pip do without Herbert? He gives Pip somewhere to live, listens to him moan, helps hide Magwitch, and then saves Pip's life. In an essay, you could compare his caring nature to Joe's or Biddy's.

Analysis of Volume Three: Chapters 54-56

This is crunch time — all the boys have to do is fetch Magwitch without being seen, row him halfway down the Thames, catch a ferry in the middle of the Thames estuary and not get nicked by the police. Simple.

The escape attempt fails

KEY EVENT

1) Just when it looks like the escape plan will be a success, a boat full of men come to arrest Magwitch. Compeyson is one of the men. Magwitch grabs him and both men fall into the river. Only Magwitch comes back up — he's badly injured and Compeyson has drowned.

Theme — Crime and Justice

Jack, a man from the nearby pub, leads the search for Compeyson's body. He only wants to steal his clothes. This undignified end is Compeyson getting what he deserves.

2) Magwitch is arrested and taken back to London. Pip doesn't think the legal system will treat Magwitch fairly because of his past, so he thinks it might be better for him to die from his injuries. Dickens is criticising the justice system at the time.

3) Pip's feelings towards Magwitch have completely changed — "my repugnance to him had all melted away". He promises to stay with Magwitch no matter what happens next.

Herbert and Wemmick look forward to new lives

Theme — Relationships

In these chapters Pip is aware of the "dull sense of being alone". He's being left behind by a lot of the people who care about him.

1) Herbert offers Pip a job working for his firm in Egypt. It's as if Pip's being rewarded for using his money in a good way by getting Herbert the job in the first place.

2) Wemmick marries Mrs Skiffins and Pip's his best man. There are a couple of funny moments as the Aged P tries to get his gloves on, and because he can't hear what the clergyman is saying. This lightens the mood of some pretty grim chapters.

Magwitch dies in jail

KEY EVENT

1) Magwitch's injuries are so bad that he's allowed to live in the prison infirmary (hospital). Pip visits him as often as he can, talking to him and reading to him.

2) While Magwitch is sick, Pip holds his hand to comfort him. He also holds it through Magwitch's trial.

Writer's Techniques — Symbolism

Hands are important in *Great Expectations*. Estella judges Pip for his "coarse hands", Pumblechook wants to shake Pip's hand once he's rich and Pip knows from Molly's hands that she's Estella's mother. Look out for more examples in the novel.

© ITV/Rex Features

3) Magwitch's fortune and land in Australia will be confiscated by the government because he's a criminal. He doesn't know this and thinks when he dies Pip will be rich. Pip doesn't tell him the truth because he wants him to die happy.

KEY QUOTE

"O Lord, be merciful to him, a sinner!"

When Pip first meets Magwitch as a boy, he's terrified. When adult Pip meets Magwitch in London, he's disgusted. But by the time Magwitch dies, Pip loves and respects him, and he asks God to forgive him.

Analysis of Volume Three: Chapters 57-59

Well, tickle me pink and call me Pip, we're nearly there. The action and the drama are over and it's time to tie up all the loose threads of the story with some calmer, more reflective chapters and a happy-ish ending...

Pip is exhausted and becomes unwell

1) The "stress" of the escape attempt and looking after Magwitch has made Pip ill. He collapses with a fever. Two debt collectors arrive to arrest Pip for unpaid bills, but he's too unwell to move.

Writer's Techniques — Language

Dickens emphasises the fact that Joe and Pip's relationship has gone back to how it used to be by using the word "old" lots of times when he describes the way they are together.

2) When he gets better, he realises Joe has been looking after him. They seem to be returning to their old, easy ways — Pip says "I was like a child in his hands."

3) As Pip gets stronger Joe becomes more distant and he leaves as soon as Pip's better. After he's gone Pip finds a receipt that shows Joe has paid off all his debts. Dickens is contrasting Joe and Pip — Joe has never had much money, but he was sensible and saved it up. Pip was rich, but wasted his money and got into debt.

Pip goes to Kent... then Egypt

1) Pip has finally realised that he would be happy if he married Biddy. He goes down to Kent to propose to her. He's still arrogant enough to just assume she'll say yes.

2) At the forge Pip finds Joe and Biddy on their wedding day. He's disappointed, but he's now mature enough to be happy for them and realise that they suit each other.

3) Pip goes to Egypt and works hard to pay off his debts. Now he's actually earning his money instead of just being given it.

© Robert Brookes

Pip and Estella meet again

KEY EVENT

1) After eleven years, Pip returns to the forge. Joe and Biddy have a daughter and a son called Pip. Young Pip is sitting by the fire with Joe just like Old Pip used to. The unhappy family of Mrs Joe, Joe and Pip has been replaced by a much happier version — Joe, Biddy, New Pip and his sister. Dickens makes sure that the really good characters in the novel — Joe and Biddy — get a proper happy ending.

2) Pip bumps into Estella at Satis House. He's heard that Bentley Drummle was a violent husband but died two years earlier. Estella says she's often thought of Pip and hopes they can be friends. Pip takes her hand and they leave together. Pip believes they won't part again but it's not very clear from the ending.

In the original ending, Pip and Estella meet when Estella's already remarried to someone else — they definitely don't get together. One of Dickens's friends persuaded him to change it as it was too depressing.

EXAM TIP

Write about how Dickens creates a satisfying ending...

Whether you like Dickens or not, you've got to admit it's satisfying that his characters get what they deserve, especially that nasty Drummle. You could write about the effect that Dickens' endings have on the reader.

Practice Questions

Now you've read the whole of this section, you should know pretty much everything that happens in 'Great Expectations'. Use these questions to check it's all sunk deep into your brain and if it hasn't, have another read.

Quick Questions

1) Where is Pip when he's attacked by the convict?

2) What happens at the end of Chapter Four to make it a cliffhanger?

3) What two things about Satis House make it seem like a prison?

4) What does the strange man in the pub give Pip in Chapter Ten?

5) Why does Miss Havisham give Joe money in Chapter Thirteen?

6) How does Dickens hint that danger is coming just before Mrs Joe's attacked?

7) Who tells Pip about his "great expectations"?

8) Who does Pip move in with in London?

9) What's the name of Jaggers' housekeeper?

10) How does Pip get Orlick sacked?

Practice Questions

And here, for your delight and entertainment, are some more questions... Well, maybe they won't give you delight or entertainment, but they will help you to find out what you've remembered from Section Two...

Quick Questions

1) Where does Wemmick take Pip while he's waiting for Estella in Chapter 32?

2) What does Pip promise Biddy after Mrs Joe's funeral?

3) What nice thing does Pip do for Herbert when he gets his birthday money?

4) What animal does Pip compare Magwitch to when he's eating in Chapter 40?

5) Why did Magwitch get a harsher sentence than Compeyson when they were on trial?

6) What does Wemmick's note say at the end of Chapter 44?

7) Who are Estella's parents?

8) Why did Jaggers give Estella to Miss Havisham?

9) What will happen to Magwitch's money after he dies?

10) Apart from taking care of him, what else does Joe do for Pip in Chapter 57?

Character Profile — Pip

Pip's life, from the age of about seven into his thirties, is the story of *Great Expectations*. That makes him the most important character by miles. Time to get to know him better...

Pip is the most important character

© Robert Brookes

1) Pip is the <u>main character</u> (protagonist) of the novel. All the action centres around <u>Pip</u> and his <u>experiences</u>.

> **Pip is...**
>
> **Ambitious:** "I want to be a gentleman."
>
> **Snobbish:** "I wanted to make Joe less ignorant and common".
>
> **Kind:** "I wished my own good fortune to reflect some rays upon him".

2) Pip's also the <u>narrator</u>, telling the story <u>years afterward</u>, from his point of view as an <u>adult</u>.

3) Pip the <u>narrator</u> is <u>looking back</u> at his younger self, and understands things <u>better</u> than he did at the time. He sounds <u>wiser</u> and more <u>mature</u> than the younger Pip. For example, when Joe visits Pip in Chapter 27:

> **Pip's Thoughts — At The Time**
>
> "he fell into such <u>unaccountable</u> fits of meditation... and dropped so much more than he ate... that I was <u>heartily glad</u> when Herbert left".

> **Pip's Thoughts — Looking Back**
>
> "I had neither the good sense nor the good feeling to know that this was <u>all my fault</u>... if I had been easier with Joe, Joe would have been easier with me."

Pip starts life innocent and naive

> **Character — Mrs Joe**
>
> Pip's sister constantly <u>criticises</u> him, and she <u>hits</u> him. This makes the reader feel <u>sorry</u> for Pip.

1) Dickens introduces young Pip as a <u>sympathetic</u> character — he's a "bundle of shivers" surrounded by the <u>tombstones</u> of his parents and brothers. The reader <u>pities</u> him.

2) Pip's attitude towards Magwitch shows that he's <u>good-hearted</u>. Even though Magwitch is <u>threatening</u>, Pip feels <u>pity</u> for "his desolation" and is "<u>glad</u>" that he enjoyed the food.

3) Pip's <u>first visit to Satis House</u> shows how <u>little experience</u> he has of life outside the forge and the village. He feels "<u>uncomfortable</u>" and "<u>half afraid</u>", and is <u>easily upset</u> by Estella's teasing.

Pip becomes ambitious

1) The visit to Satis House <u>changes</u> how Pip sees himself. He feels "much more <u>ignorant</u>" and thinks his background makes him "<u>low-lived</u>".

2) Miss Havisham's <u>wealth</u> makes Pip <u>dissatisfied</u> with what he already has. Estella's <u>insults</u> make Pip feel as if he's not <u>good enough</u> — he wants to <u>improve</u> himself, and thinks that means becoming a <u>gentleman</u>.

3) This desire is <u>positive</u> in a way — he tries hard to <u>educate</u> himself. But Pip also becomes a <u>less likeable</u> character as his need to <u>escape</u> his "common" background makes him <u>critical</u> of his friends and family:

- He is "<u>ashamed</u> of home" and "<u>disgusted</u>" with his life. This makes him seem <u>ungrateful</u>.
- Pip becomes <u>snobbish</u> — he calls Joe "a <u>mere</u> blacksmith" and wants him to be "<u>worthier</u> of my society".
- He's <u>insensitive</u>, e.g. when he says to Biddy: "If I could only get myself to fall in love with you".

Character Profile — Pip

London makes Pip hard-hearted and selfish

© ITV/Rex Features

1) When Pip learns he will be <u>rich</u>, his behaviour becomes increasingly <u>snobbish</u>. E.g. he speaks to Biddy in a "<u>superior</u>" voice and <u>accuses</u> her of being "<u>envious</u>". When he moves away, he <u>doesn't</u> keep in touch.

2) Even though Pip's dreams come <u>true</u> and he becomes a <u>gentleman</u>, he still isn't <u>happy</u>. He spends a lot of money on <u>superficial</u> things like a butler and clothes, but he's "more or less <u>miserable</u>".

3) When Joe comes to see Pip the visit is <u>awkward</u> and <u>difficult</u>. It's Pip's fault — he makes <u>no effort</u> to put Joe at his ease. Instead he feels <u>embarrassed</u> by his country ways and can't wait to <u>get rid of him</u>.

Pip has some positive characteristics

Although Pip becomes <u>snobbish</u> and behaves badly towards Joe, Dickens also shows that he can be <u>kind</u> and <u>generous</u>. He's a <u>good-hearted</u> person who has some <u>flaws</u> — this makes him a more <u>realistic</u> character.

1) Pip is <u>pleasant</u> and <u>friendly</u>, and <u>gets on well</u> with most of the people he meets in London, including <u>Herbert</u> and <u>Wemmick</u>.

2) Pip shows <u>bravery</u> when he tries to help Magwitch escape.

3) Pip often feels <u>guilty</u> — he feels guilty for stealing his sister's pie, pinching Herbert's inheritance, and the way he treats Joe.

4) His feelings of guilt shows that he has a <u>strong conscience</u>. He <u>ignores</u> his conscience for most of the book, but does the right thing in the end.

Writer's Techniques — Narrative

<u>Older Pip</u> sometimes <u>comments</u> on the actions of his younger self. E.g. when <u>young</u> Pip is <u>overjoyed</u> to be leaving the village, older Pip knows this attitude was <u>selfish</u>. He refers to Joe as "dear good Joe, whom I was so ready to leave and so unthankful to".

Pip learns from his experiences

'Great Expectations' is a '<u>bildungsroman</u>' — a novel that focuses on the main character's personal and moral development as they grow from child to adult. See p.52 for more.

Several <u>events</u> happen at the end of the novel that change Pip's <u>morals</u> for the better and cure his <u>snobbery</u>:

1) Pip finds out that his money comes from <u>Magwitch</u>. This huge <u>shock</u> changes how Pip sees his 'great expectations'. He realises that he "deserted Joe" because he valued <u>anonymous wealth</u> more than <u>love</u>.

2) At first he "<u>recoiled</u>" from Magwitch because of his "savage air" and <u>coarse</u> habits. But eventually Pip learns to look past Magwitch's social status as a <u>convict</u> and recognises his <u>loyalty</u> and <u>generosity</u>.

3) When Pip becomes very ill in Chapter 57, he learns a lot from Joe. Joe's <u>kindness</u>, even after Pip has been so <u>unpleasant</u> to him, makes Pip <u>ashamed</u> of his earlier behaviour and <u>determined to do better</u>.

4) Pip finally sees that money and education aren't as important as <u>kindness</u>. He learns to be <u>thankful</u> for <u>friends</u> and <u>family</u> — when he moves to Egypt he keeps a "<u>constant correspondence</u> with Biddy and Joe."

EXAM TIP

Write about the changes in Pip's character...

Pip is interesting because he changes throughout the book. He starts well, gets worse, then ends up pulling himself together. In your essay, try to mention Pip's good <u>and</u> bad bits — and how he changes over time.

Character Profile — Estella

Estella comes across as quite a tough nut, but you have to feel slightly sorry for her growing up in Satis House with old Miss Havisham. That would be enough to turn the best of us a bit funny.

Estella is cold and cruel to men

Estella's name means 'star'. It suggests she's beautiful, but out of reach.

1) Estella has been trained by Miss Havisham to "wreak revenge on all the male sex" by attracting men, then rejecting them. She's very good at controlling men and making them do what she wants.

2) As a child, Estella uses Pip to practise on — Miss Havisham tells her to "break his heart". She makes cruel comments about Pip's working class appearance and takes "quick delight" in making him cry.

3) As an adult, Estella is totally honest with Pip. She flirts with men to "deceive and entrap" them, but tells Pip to "take warning" and refuses to lead him on. This is a hint that she doesn't enjoy being a heartbreaker.

> **Estella is...**
>
> **Beautiful:** "beautiful and self-possessed"
>
> **Cold:** "I have no heart"
>
> **Critical:** "Her contempt for me was so strong, that it became infectious"

4) However, Estella doesn't take any responsibility for her cold-hearted behaviour. She blames Miss Havisham completely — "What?... do you reproach me for being cold? You?... I am what you have made me."

5) In Chapter 59 she's open and affectionate — she greets Pip with a "friendly touch" and says he has "a place in my heart". This suggests that she became a nicer person when she was free from Miss Havisham's influence.

Estella represents wealth and sophistication

© Moviestore Collection Ltd

1) Estella represents everything Pip wants and can't have. She's sophisticated, rich, and unobtainable — just as education and wealth seem out of Pip's grasp.

2) Estella's upper class upbringing doesn't make her happy — her rich adoptive mother damages her emotionally, and her rich husband abuses her. This shows that money and social status don't guarantee happiness.

3) It's ironic that Estella, who makes Pip want to be a gentleman, is from a criminal background — Pip only thinks she's upper class. This shows that his dreams are based on what appears to be true, rather than what's real.

Estella and Pip are similar in some ways

1) Estella also came from a poor background — she became upper class when Miss Havisham adopted her.

2) She rejects Pip, who is kind and loving to her. Instead, she marries violent Bentley Drummle because of his superior social class. Similarly, Pip rejects Joe's loving friendship for Estella's distant cruelty.

3) In the end, Estella learns from her experiences and becomes a nicer person, just as Pip does. She asks Pip to "tell me we are friends" and says she regrets being "quite ignorant" of Pip's "worth" as a friend.

KEY QUOTE

"I have no heart"

Estella is a character people love to hate. She's cold, stand-offish, and enjoys criticising others, especially Pip. But I'd cut her some slack — after all, she was raised by a crazy lady in a decaying wedding dress.

Character Profile — Miss Havisham

It's easy to imagine what Miss Havisham looked like — masses of crazy white hair, that yellowing wedding dress, and long bony fingers. All the better for pointing with...

Miss Havisham is obsessed with her past

1) Miss Havisham was once <u>engaged</u> to <u>Compeyson</u> (see p.39). On her wedding day he <u>didn't</u> turn up — he just <u>wanted her money</u> and was never going to marry her. She was <u>heartbroken</u>, and never recovered.

2) Dickens uses <u>strong imagery</u> to show how unhealthily <u>obsessed</u> Miss Havisham is with her own despair:

- She's worn her "withered" <u>wedding dress</u> every day since being jilted.

- She keeps the <u>mouldy wedding cake</u> out — it's covered with insects and "black fungus".

- All the clocks say it's 8.40 (the <u>time when she was jilted</u>) — she hasn't moved on.

> **Miss Havisham is...**
>
> **Cruel:** "horribly cruel... to torture me through all these years"
>
> **Mad:** "her mind... had grown diseased"
>
> **Bitter:** "love is... unquestioning self-humiliation"

> **Writer's Techniques — Symbolism**
>
> Just like Miss Havisham, everything in Satis House is <u>broken</u>, <u>decaying</u> and <u>isolated</u>. Everything that used to be white "was <u>faded</u> and <u>yellow</u>".

Miss Havisham uses Estella and Pip

1) She invites Pip to Satis House to give the young Estella some practice in <u>manipulating men</u>. When Estella says she doesn't want to play cards with Pip, Miss Havisham replies: "Well? You can <u>break</u> his <u>heart</u>."

2) Miss Havisham is <u>delighted</u> when Pip falls in love with Estella. This shows how <u>cruel</u> she is — she <u>wants</u> Pip to get hurt and doesn't care about his <u>feelings</u>.

3) Dickens uses her character to show how <u>dangerous</u> obsession is. Miss Havisham's obsessive need for <u>revenge</u> ruins her life, but it also <u>damages</u> Pip and Estella, and <u>changes</u> their lives forever.

© Nigel Norrington/ArenaPAL

She eventually changes her ways

> **Character — Pip**
>
> Pip's attitude to Miss Havisham shows that he can be <u>forgiving</u>. He tells her to "<u>dismiss</u> me from your mind and conscience", even though she <u>manipulated</u> and <u>lied</u> to him.

1) In Chapter 49, Miss Havisham realises she's <u>made Pip suffer</u> in exactly the <u>same way</u> she has suffered: "'O!' she cried, despairingly. 'What have I done! What have I done!'"

2) Just like Pip, she <u>achieves</u> her <u>dream</u>, but it doesn't make her <u>happy</u>. This highlights Dickens' message that following dreams that are <u>purely selfish</u> doesn't make people happy.

3) She becomes a <u>weak</u>, <u>pitiable</u> creature who <u>begs</u> Pip for forgiveness "on her knees" and is <u>desperate</u> to do "something useful and good". Her <u>regret</u> makes the reader feel <u>sorry</u> for her, rather than <u>blame</u> her.

KEY QUOTE

"Love her, love her, love her!"

I think Miss Havisham's the best character — she's one of the most crazy, brilliant inventions in all of fiction. She's cruel, manipulative, and pretty unrealistic, but somehow the reader ends up sympathising with her...

Character Profile — Magwitch

Hmmm... seems to be a pattern emerging here. Like Miss Havisham, Estella and Pip, Magwitch has a bad and good side. And like the others, he shows his good side before the fat lady sings.

Magwitch is terrifying when he first appears

1) At first, Magwitch comes across as a <u>violent</u> and <u>aggressive</u> character.

2) Pip describes him as "A <u>fearful</u> man, all in coarse grey, with a great iron on his leg" who <u>threatens</u> that "your heart and your liver shall be <u>tore out</u>, roasted, and ate."

Magwitch is...

Violent: "Keep still, you little devil, or I'll cut your throat!"
Hard-working: "I worked hard, that you should be above work."
Loyal: "great constancy through a series of years"

3) But even at this point in the novel, there are <u>hints</u> that Magwitch has <u>good qualities</u>. He doesn't actually <u>harm</u> Pip, and he <u>lies</u> to <u>protect</u> him, telling the soldiers that he stole the <u>food</u> and <u>file</u> from the forge.

4) Whenever Pip sees other criminals, he's <u>reminded</u> of the convict in the graveyard. He thinks of Magwitch as a <u>threatening presence</u> who has tainted him with a "stain" of <u>criminality</u> "that was faded but not gone".

Magwitch's true nature is revealed

1) In Chapter 39, Magwitch reappears to <u>reveal</u> he "made a <u>gentlemen</u>" of Pip.

2) Magwitch's <u>determination</u> to reward Pip for <u>helping</u> him on the marshes, and <u>desperation</u> to do something <u>good</u>, show that he's <u>moral</u> and <u>generous</u>.

3) Magwitch's kindness to Pip is also partly motivated by his desire to get <u>revenge</u> on society for the way he's been treated. He shouts "blast you every one, from the <u>judge</u>... to the <u>colonist</u>... I'll show a <u>better gentleman</u> than the whole kit on you put together!"

Theme — Crime and Justice

Dickens uses <u>Magwitch's</u> story to highlight the message that many <u>criminals</u> are <u>good</u>, <u>kind</u> people in <u>unfortunate</u> situations, or who have just made <u>mistakes</u>.

Pip grows to love Magwitch

1) At first, <u>Pip's</u> reaction on discovering that Magwitch gave him his fortune is <u>snobbish</u> and <u>ungrateful</u>. He can't see Magwitch as anything other than "<u>Prisoner</u>, <u>Felon</u>, <u>Bondsman</u>". Pip's behaviour makes the reader feel <u>sorry</u> for Magwitch, because they can see his <u>true</u>, <u>good</u> nature.

2) When Pip hears Magwitch's story, and realises he is Estella's father, he learns to see Magwitch as a <u>true friend</u> who "had felt... <u>gratefully</u>, and <u>generously</u>, towards me", instead of as a <u>convict</u>.

3) As Magwitch is dying Pip <u>prays</u>, "O Lord, be merciful to him a sinner!" Magwitch has taught Pip that <u>compassion</u> and <u>human kindness</u> are far more important than <u>social status</u>.

Write about why Magwitch is important in the novel...

He's more of a hairy godmother than a fairy one, but Magwitch is a really important part of Pip's life story — which makes him important to the plot of the novel, too. Magwitch's actions drive the plot forwards.

Character Profile — Joe

Joe is a bit different to the characters we've seen so far. He's pretty much an all-round top bloke and good egg.

Joe treats Pip like a son

1) Joe stands out as the one character in Pip's life who <u>looks after</u> him and loves him <u>like his own son</u>. He's always <u>loyal</u> and <u>supportive</u> to Pip.

2) But even as a boy Pip doesn't fully <u>respect</u> Joe. He sees him "as a larger species of <u>child</u>, and as no more than my <u>equal</u>".

3) Pip soon begins to <u>look down on</u> Joe because he isn't rich or educated. Pip thinks these are the things that make you a <u>gentleman</u>. Joe knows this, but he never gets angry with Pip — which shows how <u>understanding</u> Joe is.

> **Joe is...**
>
> **Nice:** "mild, good-natured, sweet-tempered, easy-going"
> **Forgiving:** "God knows as I forgive you, if I have anythink to forgive!"
> **Strong but gentle:** "the steam-hammer that can crush a man or pat an egg-shell, in his combination of strength with gentleness."

4) Although Joe isn't a <u>gentleman</u> in terms of his social class, he is a <u>gentleman</u> in the way he <u>behaves</u>. He's <u>honest</u>, <u>patient</u> and <u>kind</u>. Dickens uses Joe to show what qualities <u>really matter</u>, and Pip's treatment of Joe shows very clearly that <u>Pip</u> doesn't <u>understand</u> what is <u>important</u> in life.

Joe is intelligent but uneducated, and strong but gentle

1) On the surface Joe doesn't seem too bright. He <u>stumbles</u> over his <u>words</u> and he <u>can't read</u> and write. But he says some very <u>wise</u> things, and expresses himself <u>well</u> when he's <u>confident</u> of what he's saying.

2) Joe has <u>physical strength</u> but he's <u>not violent</u>. Mrs Joe hits him but he <u>doesn't fight back</u>.

3) Joe's <u>strength</u> contrasts with his <u>gentle</u> nature, and his clumsy <u>speech</u> contrasts with his <u>wise</u> thoughts. Dickens uses these contrasts to highlight the novel's message that <u>appearances</u> don't <u>matter</u> — it's what's <u>beneath</u> the surface that <u>counts</u>.

Joe's personality contrasts with Pip's

1) Unlike Pip, Joe has <u>no social ambitions</u>. He <u>prefers</u> to live a hard-working, honest life, saying, "If you can't get to be oncommon through going <u>straight</u>, you'll never get to do it through going <u>crooked</u>."

2) Joe is <u>content</u> because he always focuses on the <u>positive</u>. E.g. he says his violent father was "good in his hart" and calls Mrs Joe a "fine figure of a woman". In contrast, Pip focuses on what he's <u>missing</u>, instead of <u>appreciating</u> what he <u>has</u>.

3) Joe's <u>not perfect</u> though — he <u>fails</u> to <u>protect</u> Pip from Mrs Joe's <u>abuse</u>. This shows that there's a <u>weak</u> side to his character.

Mention Dickens' use of repeated phrases...

The examiner will be looking for points about language. One way that Dickens makes his characters stick in your mind is by giving them catchphrases — Joe's top phrases are "ever the best of friends" and "what larks".

Character Profile — Biddy

Biddy is another of the near-perfect characters in the book. Like Joe she's an all-round good 'un. She pulls off the excellent trick of being nice to people without being wet or a doormat. Go Biddy.

Biddy sets Pip a good example

1) Biddy is <u>kind</u> to Pip and gives him <u>extra help</u> at school. It's also suggested that she <u>loves</u> Pip — she shows "<u>deep concern</u> in everything" he tells her.

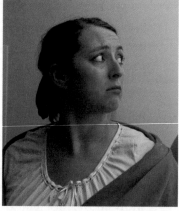

© Robert Brookes

> **Biddy is...**
>
> **Kind:** "she would far rather have wounded her own breast than mine."
> **Sensible:** "Biddy was the wisest of girls".
> **Determined:** "I can be industrious and patient, and teach myself".

2) Biddy isn't afraid to <u>criticise</u> Pip — in this way, she acts as Pip's <u>conscience</u>:

- Pip tells Biddy that he wants to be a <u>gentleman</u> because of Estella. She replies that if Estella calls Pip <u>common</u> then she's "<u>not worth</u> gaining over" and "<u>caring nothing</u> for her" would make Pip <u>happier</u>.

- When Pip makes <u>patronising comments</u> about Joe, Biddy tries to explain that Joe might <u>not want</u> to be 'improved'. This shows that she's more <u>understanding</u> and <u>accepting</u> than Pip.

- When Pip promises to visit Joe, she <u>openly</u> voices her <u>doubts</u>: "Are you quite sure, then, that you WILL come to see him often?"

3) Pip <u>ignores</u> her advice — just as he <u>ignores</u> his conscience and doesn't do what he <u>knows deep down</u> is <u>right</u>.

Biddy's goals are realistic — and she achieves them all

1) Biddy is a bit <u>like Pip</u> in that she wants a <u>better life</u>. But her idea of a better life is a <u>good job</u> and <u>home</u>. The contrast shows that Pip's dreams are <u>extravagant</u> and <u>unrealistic</u>.

> **Theme — Relationships**
>
> It's <u>hinted</u> that Biddy was in love with Pip, but she <u>moves on</u>, and finds happiness with Joe. This contrasts with Pip and Miss Havisham — who both make themselves <u>miserable</u> by <u>obsessing</u> about someone they <u>can't have</u>.

2) Biddy is <u>active</u> and <u>determined</u> — she makes the most of <u>every opportunity</u> and works very hard to become a teacher. In contrast, Pip is <u>passive</u> — he <u>waits</u> for Miss Havisham to make him a gentleman.

3) Through Biddy, Dickens shows that <u>education</u> is <u>valuable</u>. She <u>enjoys</u> learning for its <u>own sake</u>, and puts her education to <u>good use</u> by becoming a <u>teacher</u>.

4) When Pip eventually <u>recognises</u> Biddy's <u>good qualities</u> and goes to propose, he finds that she's married Joe. Dickens makes it clear that this is the happy ending Biddy <u>deserves</u>. She speaks in a "<u>burst</u> of <u>happiness</u>" and says she "couldn't <u>love</u> him better".

> **Character — Estella**
>
> There's a <u>strong contrast</u> between the characters of Biddy and Estella. Estella's <u>cruel</u> to Pip but wins his heart. Biddy <u>respects</u> Pip, but he <u>doesn't appreciate</u> her. Biddy's life is hard — but she's <u>grateful</u> for what she has, unlike Estella.

KEY QUOTE

"she was pleasant and wholesome and sweet-tempered."

Lovely Biddy is like a female version of Joe — patient, hard-working and kind. It's almost like they were made for each other. Hang on — they <u>were</u> made for each other. That Dickens was one smart cookie...

Character Profile — Mrs Joe and Pumblechook

Mrs Joe and Pumblechook are a fine pair. I'm not going to say they're completely unbearable, but... well... let's say you wouldn't want to be stuck in a lift with either of them for too long.

Mrs Joe is a rampaging tyrant

© Robert Brookes

1) Mrs Joe likes to say she has raised Pip "<u>by hand</u>". This means she bottle-fed him when he was a baby. It also suggests a lot of <u>beatings</u>, and Pip says she has a "<u>hard</u> and <u>heavy</u> hand".

2) Dickens uses <u>imagery</u> to develop her character — she wears an apron "stuck full of <u>pins</u> and <u>needles</u>" and is "<u>bony</u>". These descriptions suggest she is <u>sharp</u>, prickly and <u>unfriendly</u>.

Theme — Ambition

Mrs Joe wants to <u>improve</u> her <u>social status</u> — she complains that "It's <u>bad enough</u> to be a blacksmith's wife". Her <u>ambition</u> makes her <u>cruelly judgemental</u> of kindhearted Joe.

3) Mrs Joe's anger and violence end up <u>ruining her life</u>. Orlick insults her and she "<u>deliberately</u>" becomes hysterical, <u>encouraging</u> Joe to beat him up. Orlick attacks her in <u>revenge</u>, leaving her <u>brain-damaged</u>.

4) Mrs Joe changes after the attack — Dickens may be suggesting she <u>deserved punishment</u> for mistreating Pip, and her suffering makes her a <u>better person</u>. E.g.

- Mrs Joe's memory and sight are "impaired" but her "<u>temper</u> was greatly <u>improved</u>".

- She shows "<u>anxiety</u> to be on good terms" with Orlick — suggesting she wants his <u>forgiveness</u>.

- Just before she dies, Mrs Joe seems to ask for <u>forgiveness</u> and to see her <u>husband</u> and <u>brother</u> — she only says: "Pardon", "Joe" and "Pip".

Pumblechook likes to feel important

1) Pumblechook is greedy — for <u>money</u>, <u>status</u> and <u>respect</u>. Dickens often describes Pumblechook at mealtimes, <u>eating</u> in a "<u>gorging</u>" manner or "breathing sherry and crumbs". This <u>symbolises</u> his greed.

2) When Pip is a <u>child</u>, Pumblechook looks at him with "<u>indignation</u> and <u>abhorrence</u>". But he changes his attitude when Pip inherits his <u>great expectations</u>. He calls Pip "my dear young friend" and treats him with a "<u>servile</u> manner". But he soon asks for "more capital" — he's <u>only</u> interested in Pip's <u>money</u>.

3) Pumblechook <u>brags</u> to everyone that he was Pip's "earliest <u>patron</u>" and the "<u>founder</u>" of his fortune — but he <u>wasn't</u>. This <u>contrasts</u> with Joe, who loved and looked after Pip, but never wanted <u>public credit</u> for it.

Theme — Social Class

Pumblechook's greed and hypocrisy are <u>exaggerated</u> to add <u>humour</u> to the novel, but Dickens also uses them to <u>criticise</u> the importance placed on <u>wealth</u> and <u>social class</u> in society at that time.

4) Joe and Magwitch also <u>forgive</u> Pip for being ungrateful, but Pumblechook <u>publicly</u> accuses him of having a "total <u>deficiency</u> of common human <u>gratitoode</u>".

Describe how Dickens creates engaging characters...

You can write about how Dickens doesn't just describe Mrs Joe or Pumblechook as complete monsters — Mrs Joe changes, and there's humour in the way Pumblechook speaks, which makes them more interesting.

Character Profile — Jaggers, Wemmick and Molly

Jaggers is the scary lawyer who looks after Miss Havisham's and Pip's legal and financial affairs. Wemmick is his clerk and Molly is his mysterious housekeeper. They're all pretty odd in their own special ways.

Jaggers is a top-notch lawyer

© Robert Brookes

1) Jaggers is a <u>lawyer</u> who defends people in the <u>criminal courts</u>. He's so <u>powerful</u> and <u>feared</u> that he doesn't have to lock his doors at night — no criminal in London would dare to rob him.

2) Jaggers doesn't <u>understand</u> why Joe <u>won't</u> accept money as <u>compensation</u> when Pip stops being his apprentice. This makes him seem <u>cold</u> and <u>unfeeling</u>.

3) Jaggers is more worried about <u>appearances</u> than <u>honesty</u>. He knows his clients <u>lie</u> in court, and he doesn't care, as long as it <u>looks as if</u> Jaggers thinks they're telling the truth. For example, one client tells him he has a <u>fake witnesses</u> "prepared to swear... anythink". Jaggers replies "how dare you tell ME that".

4) But Jaggers has a <u>good side</u> too. He gets very <u>angry</u> about the way children are "imprisoned, whipped, transported, neglected, cast out... and growing up to be hanged".

Writer's Techniques — Symbolism

Jaggers constantly <u>washes his hands</u> — this <u>symbolises</u> his <u>conscience</u>. He wants to wash away the <u>crime</u> and <u>dishonesty</u> he is constantly in contact with.

5) He also 'saved' Estella from a life of <u>crime</u> and <u>poverty</u> and employs Molly <u>despite</u> her criminal past. He's a lot more <u>caring</u> than the reader initially thinks — this makes his character more <u>balanced</u> and <u>believable</u>.

Wemmick likes to hide his true feelings

Writer's Techniques — Symbolism

Wemmick's house <u>symbolises</u> his need to <u>protect</u> his personal life from his life in London. He <u>refuses</u> to discuss his home-life, and built a <u>castle</u> to keep it safe. This suggests the city is <u>dangerous</u>.

1) At home in Walworth, Wemmick is <u>jolly</u>, <u>warm</u> and <u>caring</u>. He has close and <u>loving relationships</u> with <u>Miss Skiffins</u> and his elderly, deaf father, the <u>Aged Parent</u>.

2) But in the office, Wemmick conforms to society's expectations of a "professional" clerk — he's <u>cold and unemotional</u>, with a "wooden face" and a mouth like a "<u>post-office</u>".

3) Dickens uses Wemmick to <u>criticise</u> the <u>values</u> of society at the time. The two sides to his personality show that people often <u>change</u> for the <u>worse</u> when they try to fit in to <u>society</u>.

Molly the housekeeper is Estella's mother

1) Jaggers' housekeeper is described as "a wild beast <u>tamed</u>". She's <u>withdrawn</u>, with strangely <u>strong</u> wrists.

2) It's obvious that Molly has a <u>dark</u> and <u>interesting</u> history, but it's not revealed until near the <u>end</u> of the novel. This adds <u>mystery</u> and <u>suspense</u> as the reader wonders how she fits into the plot.

Writer's Techniques — Symbolism

Like many hands in the novel, Molly's <u>hands</u> are symbolic. Pip realises Molly and Estella are <u>related</u> because their hands are <u>similar</u>.

3) Eventually, Pip realises Molly is <u>Estella's mother</u>. Jaggers wanted to <u>save Estella</u> from her mother's rough, criminal life, and persuaded Molly to give Estella up for <u>adoption</u>.

KEY QUOTE

"when I come into the Castle, I leave the office behind me."

Wemmick is one of the nicest characters in the book. Who needs the luxury of Satis House or Jaggers' home, when you can visit Wemmick's mini-castle, with his sweet old dad and piles of toast and sausages.

Character Profile — Compeyson, Orlick & Drummle

Jaggers is a bit creepy, but these three are definitely bad to the bone. Compeyson is Magwitch's enemy, and later Pip's. Orlick hates Pip and tries to kill him. Drummle is Pip's main rival for Estella. What a scary set...

Compeyson is a ruthless criminal

1) Compeyson is the <u>second convict</u> in the marshes — the one Pip surprises as he brings food for Magwitch.

2) Compeyson and Magwitch used to run a forgery scam <u>together</u>, but they're now <u>huge enemies</u>.

3) Dickens creates <u>contrasts</u> between the two <u>convicts</u>, to show that not all criminals are <u>equally bad</u>:

- Compeyson is from an <u>upper class</u> background and <u>chose</u> to be a criminal. This contrasts with Magwitch, who never really <u>wanted</u> to be a criminal, but had to steal to <u>survive</u>.

- Compeyson <u>manipulated</u> and <u>controlled</u> Magwitch, so when they were prosecuted, all the evidence was against Magwitch and Compeyson was <u>crafty</u> enough to make himself look <u>less guilty</u>.

- Compeyson <u>jilted</u> Miss Havisham — their engagement was a <u>scam</u> to get <u>money</u> from her. This reinforces the idea that Compeyson is a <u>cruel</u> man. In comparison, Magwitch never <u>hurt</u> others if he could help it.

> **Theme — Social Class**
>
> Compeyson's <u>class protects</u> him from the <u>law</u>. He gets much less jail time than Magwitch because Compeyson was "<u>well brought up</u>" and had influential "<u>schoolfellows</u>".

Orlick is Joe's assistant at the forge

1) Orlick is <u>lazy</u>, <u>ignorant</u> and <u>violent</u>.

2) Dickens uses Orlick to add suspense and drama to Pip's story. He <u>fights with Joe</u>, and attacks <u>Mrs Joe</u> — although it's not proven straight away.

3) Orlick is <u>jealous</u> of Pip. At the forge, Orlick thinks Pip "was favoured, and he was <u>bullied</u> and <u>beat</u>". Also, Orlick likes Biddy but she <u>prefers</u> Pip.

4) Orlick tries to <u>kill Pip</u>. This is a very <u>melodramatic</u> scene, and also adds <u>suspense</u> as Orlick knows about Magwitch — which puts the <u>escape plans</u> in danger.

Bentley Drummle is an upper-class bully

1) Drummle's another 'gentleman' who <u>doesn't deserve</u> the name. He's "<u>idle</u>, <u>proud</u>... and <u>suspicious</u>".

2) Jaggers says Drummle's "one of the true sort", meaning he has a truly <u>criminal</u> personality. Jaggers <u>warns Pip</u> to stay away from him.

3) Dickens uses Drummle as a <u>plot device</u>. It's hinted that his "<u>cruelty</u>" to Estella during their <u>marriage</u> is one of the things that leaves her "<u>bent</u> and <u>broken</u>" and causes her to become a more <u>sympathetic</u> character.

> **Theme — Crime and Justice**
>
> Drummle is <u>killed</u> in an accident with a horse he mistreated. This seems to be a <u>just punishment</u> for the bad things he's done.

Write about these characters' motivations...

For someone who's supposed to be nice, Pip has lots of enemies. Make sure you know their backgrounds, and why they've got it in for Pip, so you can show that you understand <u>why</u> characters act like they do.

Character Profile — The Pockets

This is starting to feel like a party, where you keep meeting people and don't have time to remember one person's name before you meet another one... At least this lot all have the same surname.

Herbert Pocket is Pip's best friend

1) Herbert and Pip meet when they are <u>boys</u> at Satis House. They have a <u>fight</u>, but later they share a flat and become <u>best friends</u>.

2) Herbert teaches Pip how he should <u>behave</u> if he wants to come across as a gentleman. He does this <u>sensitively</u>, without hurting Pip's pride — which shows that he is <u>kind</u> and not a <u>snob</u>.

3) Herbert doesn't have a <u>fortune</u> like Pip — he has to find a job and <u>work</u> for a living. He quickly gets into <u>debt</u> because of Pip's extravagant habits. This suggests he's <u>easily led</u> and a bit <u>naive</u>.

© ITV/Rex Features

> ### Herbert is...
>
> **A true gentleman**: "no man who was not a true gentleman at heart ever was... a true gentleman in manner... no varnish can hide the grain of the wood"
>
> **Kind**: "a natural incapacity to do anything secret and mean"

4) Pip's <u>friendship</u> with Herbert reveals a <u>lot</u> about <u>Pip</u>:

- To help Herbert, Pip secretly pays to set him up as a partner in a <u>shipping business</u>. This shows that although Pip can be <u>cold</u> and <u>snobbish</u>, he's still capable of being "<u>devilish good</u>".

- It also creates <u>similarities</u> between Pip and Magwitch. They both do <u>very generous</u> things <u>secretly</u> to <u>repay</u> an act of kindness or friendship, and they both feel "<u>triumph</u>" in the effect it has on the other person.

> ### Theme — Relationships
>
> Herbert has a <u>fiancée</u> called Clara. She isn't rich or titled, but Herbert truly loves her. Their relationship is based on <u>kindness</u> and <u>mutual respect</u>. It's very different from Pip's relationship with Estella.

There are lots more Pockets in the story

The fact that Matthew Pocket and Biddy are good teachers suggests that Dickens thought that education was important, even though he made Mr Wopsle's great-aunt's school seem ridiculous.

1) <u>Herbert's dad</u>, Matthew Pocket, is <u>Miss Havisham's cousin</u> and <u>Pip's tutor</u>. He's <u>kind</u>, <u>patient</u> and <u>honest</u>. He's one of the few Pockets who doesn't <u>flatter</u> or <u>lie</u> to Miss Havisham in the hope of inheriting her <u>money</u>.

2) <u>Mrs Pocket</u> is obsessed with <u>class</u> and <u>social standing</u>. She spends her time reading books "all about titles" instead of looking after her children, so the house is <u>chaotic</u> and <u>badly</u> looked after. She makes people who are obsessed with social class look <u>ridiculous</u>.

3) All the Pockets except Matthew and Herbert are <u>desperate</u> to <u>inherit</u> Miss Havisham's fortune so they <u>flatter</u> her and <u>pretend</u> to care about her — this makes them seem <u>greedy</u> and <u>foolish</u>. In the end, she doesn't leave them much in her <u>will</u> — like lots of characters in the novel, they get what they <u>deserve</u> in the end.

KEY QUOTE

"of the same blood, but... not of the same nature."

There are lots of members of the Pocket family in the novel, but Herbert and his dad are by far the nicest. Their niceness pays off thanks to Pip, who makes Miss Havisham realise that they deserve her money.

Practice Questions

If I were a Dickens character I'd be called Eunice Writeychattersworth or Betty Unfunnybottom. Get through this fine batch of practice questions and you'll be Timmy Topmarks or Susy Examsuccess.

Quick Questions

1) Who is the narrator of *Great Expectations*?

2) What has Estella been trained to do by Miss Havisham?

3) Describe Miss Havisham's everyday outfit.

4) What lie does Magwitch tell to help Pip at the beginning of the story?

5) Is Joe   a) strong and caring   or,   b) snobbish and cruel?

6) Give two differences between Biddy and Estella.

7) What does Pumblechook brag about once Pip is rich?

8) Where does Wemmick show his true personality?

9) Why does Compeyson get much less jail time than Magwitch?

10) Give two examples which suggest that Herbert is a decent and good character.

Practice Questions

These questions are a bit more like the ones you'll get in the exam. Do a written answer for each one, but don't try to tackle all the exam-style questions in one go.

In-depth Questions

1) What do you think are the key experiences that help turn Pip from a naive child into a mature adult?

2) Briefly explain what Estella represents in the novel.

3) Give one similarity and one difference between the characters of Magwitch and Joe.

4) How does Dickens make Mrs Joe and Pumblechook seem comical as well as unpleasant?

5) Write a paragraph explaining whether you think Dickens portrays Jaggers as more of a bad character or a good character.

Exam-style Questions

1) How does Dickens make you feel differently about Pip's behaviour in two different chapters of the novel?

2) Explain how Dickens presents the relationship between Pip and Estella in Chapter 33.

3) How is the character of Miss Havisham presented as sometimes cruel and sometimes pathetic in different parts of the novel?

4) Explain how Dickens presents the character of Magwitch in Chapter 56.

5) Explain how Dickens uses speech to bring out the personalities of two different characters in the novel.

Social Class

Howdy, hello, and welcome to the fourth section of the book — it's about themes. Dickens' books are famous for the way they describe everyone, from urchins to toffs, so let's dive in with a bit about social class...

Being rich isn't the same as being good

1) Social class was very important in the 1800s (see p.9). Dickens writes about characters from all social classes — e.g. Miss Havisham is upper class, Jaggers is middle class and Joe is working class.

2) *Great Expectations* explores what it means to be a gentleman. Pip learns that being a true gentleman is about showing kindness and respect rather than having wealth and status.

3) For example, Compeyson is upper class but probably the worst crook in the story. On the other hand, Magwitch is a "warmint" but has a good side.

Pip's treated differently when he's rich and when he's poor

Some characters in *Great Expectations* start treating Pip differently when they find out about his "expectations". It's through these experiences that Pip learns "the stupendous power of money".

1) Mr Pumblechook calls Pip "boy" and Pip says he would "rumple my hair" but when Pip's rich he calls him "my dear young friend" and can't stop shaking his hand.

2) The tailor doesn't think it's "worth his while" to approach Pip in his shop when he thinks he's poor, but as soon as Pip tells him about his fortune he can't do enough for Pip.

> When he's lost his money, Pip stays at the Blue Boar inn. His "usual bedroom" is full so he only gets a room "among the pigeons". He says that his normal room is probably being used by "some one who had expectations". He's treated very differently now he's not rich any more.

Upper class people care a lot about appearances

1) The upper class characters in *Great Expectations* care about appearances. Miss Havisham's relative Camilla complains about a man whose wife died and who didn't make his children wear "the deepest of trimmings" on their mourning clothes. This obsession with the way things look shows how upper class characters can be shallow and ridiculous.

2) When Pip buys new, expensive clothes to travel to London in, they don't fit him properly — they're "rather a disappointment". This shows that Pip doesn't fit in with upper class society — he doesn't belong.

Dickens often satirises (makes fun of) people who are obsessed with social class. See p.52.

Write about how Pip's attitude to class changes...

You could write about how, at the beginning of the novel, Pip likes the idea of being a gentleman from a higher social class. But by the end of the novel he changes his mind — he's happy to work for a living.

Ambition

The next theme is ambition — lots of the characters in *Great Expectations* are ambitious and Dickens uses them to show that ambition isn't always a good thing if it makes you forget your roots and your friends.

Many characters have ambitions to go up in society

1) Lots of the characters in *Great Expectations* are <u>ambitious</u> to go up in society. Pip wanting to become a <u>gentleman</u> is the main example, but <u>Mr Pumblechook</u>, <u>Mr Wopsle</u> and the <u>Pockets</u> are ambitious too.

2) After the <u>Industrial Revolution</u> in England (see p.6) it became <u>easier</u> for people to move up in society by making <u>money</u> in the new industries. This led to people being more <u>ambitious</u> because they could change their social class by <u>working hard</u> to become rich.

Ambitious characters use each other

© ITV/Rex Features

1) Mr Pumblechook wants to mix with the <u>top level</u> of <u>society</u>. He's keen to take Pip to <u>Satis House</u> because he hopes he'll be invited in and get to meet <u>Miss Havisham</u>.

2) The <u>Pocket family</u> (apart from Matthew and Herbert) are <u>social climbers</u> and <u>suck up</u> to Miss Havisham because they hope to <u>inherit</u> her money.

3) Several characters <u>use Pip</u> to get ahead in society:

- <u>Mr Pumblechook</u> arranges for Pip to <u>visit Miss Havisham</u> even though he knows that she's a <u>strange</u> and <u>scary woman</u>.
- <u>Mrs Joe</u> takes all the <u>money</u> that Pip's given when he's young and makes him go back to <u>Miss Havisham's</u> house to try to get <u>more</u>.

To go up in society you had to be educated

Many characters realise that to <u>improve</u> your <u>social status</u> you need to get an <u>education</u>.

1) Joe says that <u>Mrs Joe</u> wouldn't want him to be <u>educated</u> "for fear as I might rise" — she might <u>lose control</u> of him.

2) <u>Pip's</u> desperate to become <u>more educated</u> so that he can become a <u>gentleman</u>, and win Estella's love. As Pip becomes <u>more educated</u>, he becomes <u>arrogant</u> and starts to see himself as <u>superior</u> to Joe and the people he grew up with.

3) However, education can be a <u>good</u> thing — e.g. <u>Biddy</u> uses her education to <u>teach other people</u>.

> **Writer's Techniques**
>
> Dickens <u>questions</u> the idea that education is <u>always</u> a <u>good</u> thing by making some of his most <u>educated</u> characters very <u>unpleasant</u>. For example, <u>Bentley Drummle</u> is <u>rude</u> and <u>cruel</u>, and <u>Compeyson</u> uses his education to become a <u>professional criminal</u>.

Ambition

Pip's dreams are the main point of the story. Look more closely at what happens to Pip to find out what Dickens wanted to say about ambition and social climbing.

Less ambitious characters are usually happier

1) Throughout the novel <u>Joe</u> is kind, decent, and loyal. He's <u>happy</u> to be a <u>blacksmith</u>, although he doesn't want to <u>get in the way</u> of Pip's future. He gets the <u>happy ending</u> he deserves when he marries Biddy.

2) <u>Biddy</u> doesn't spend her whole time <u>dreaming</u> about the future. Instead she concentrates on helping <u>others</u> and her life gradually improves — she gets a good <u>job</u> as a teacher and eventually <u>marries Joe</u>.

3) <u>Herbert's</u> ambition is to get a job insuring ships and then <u>work up to</u> having a "perfect fleet". Dickens wants to show that having ambition isn't necessarily a bad thing, but you've got to be prepared to <u>work hard</u>.

Ambition is Pip's driving force

1) At Satis House, <u>Estella</u> calls Pip a "<u>common</u> labouring boy" and treats him like <u>dirt</u>. He's upset by this and wants to <u>impress</u> Estella. This drives his ambition to become a <u>gentleman</u>.

2) Pip believes he needs <u>education</u>, <u>money</u> and <u>polished manners</u> to become a gentleman. He stops paying attention to things like <u>love</u>, <u>friendship</u> and <u>loyalty</u>.

Character — Pip

Dickens tries to <u>balance</u> Pip's character. He shows how Pip's <u>ambition</u> and <u>wealth</u> change him without making him so awful that the readers <u>stop caring</u>. Dickens makes the reader <u>feel sorry</u> for Pip in the opening chapters by presenting him as <u>weak</u> and <u>defenceless</u>.

© ITV/Rex Features

Happiness comes to Pip when he loses his ambitions

1) When Pip's ill, and his <u>chances</u> of being a <u>rich</u> man are <u>gone</u>, he's finally reunited with Joe and feels <u>genuinely sorry</u> for the way he's behaved.

2) Pip also has to <u>work hard</u> after he loses all his money. He goes to work in <u>Egypt</u> with Herbert. They don't make "mints of money", but they do "<u>very well</u>". Pip's <u>become</u> one of several characters in the novel like Joe and Wemmick who <u>work hard</u> and are <u>happy</u>.

Theme — Relationships

After Pip loses his ambitions he realises what's <u>really important</u> — <u>relationships</u> with people.

"I work pretty hard for a sufficient living"

And the moral is: be good, work hard and don't expect too much. It's stern stuff, but this attitude was very popular in Victorian times. Dickens' idea of a happy ending for Pip has him living "frugally" but happily.

Crime and Justice

Dickens was on a real mission to explain to his readers how he saw the world at the time. An important point he makes is that the law's not always 100% fair, or on the side of people who try to be good.

Pip is surrounded by crime

1) Magwitch <u>drags Pip</u> into his <u>criminal life</u> when he demands food in the churchyard. He makes Pip <u>steal</u> food and <u>lie</u> about it. Throughout the novel he is continually associated with crime:

© Robert Brookes

- The <u>leg iron</u> which Magwitch files off on the marshes is also the <u>weapon</u> used to <u>attack</u> Mrs Joe. It's a <u>reminder</u> of Pip's guilty feelings about helping the convict.

- Pip's village is near the <u>prison hulks</u> and he sees a "<u>gibbet</u>" on the marshes where a pirate had been <u>hung</u>. In London he lives near <u>Newgate prison</u> with its "<u>gallows</u>" where prisoners are hung. It seems as if he can't escape <u>prisons</u> and <u>hangings</u>.

- The <u>language</u> used to describe his apprenticeship is all related to crime e.g. "<u>bound</u>" and "<u>red-handed</u>".

- There are <u>two convicts</u> on the coach when Pip goes to Kent.

2) These <u>motifs</u> of crime <u>haunt</u> Pip until Magwitch reappears.

The law isn't very fair

Writer's Techniques

Dickens <u>used</u> *Great Expectations* to put across his <u>views</u> about the <u>justice system</u> — see p.7 for more.

1) The court saw Compeyson as a <u>gentleman</u> who had been <u>led astray</u> by Magwitch so he was given a shorter sentence.

2) <u>Magwitch</u> got a harsher sentence because he's <u>lower class</u> and had been to prison <u>before</u>. The judge assumed he would get into trouble <u>again</u> — he's "likely to come to worse".

Character — Jaggers

Jaggers also bends the law to <u>help people</u> escape a life of crime and misery — that's why he gave Estella to Miss Havisham for <u>adoption</u> and <u>helped Molly</u> in her murder trial.

3) Jaggers shows how <u>corrupt</u> the law can be. He's <u>popular</u> because he can get <u>guilty</u> people <u>off the hook</u>. He uses hired witnesses to give <u>false evidence</u> in court.

4) Jaggers is prepared to <u>bend the truth</u> to win a case because he wants to make money and be <u>successful</u>.

All the characters get what they deserve

Even though the <u>law</u> isn't always <u>fair</u>, everyone gets what they <u>deserve</u> in the end:

1) Magwitch <u>dies happy</u> — Pip's by his <u>side</u> and he knows his <u>daughter</u> is alive and is a lady.

2) Joe and Biddy are <u>nice</u> throughout the novel and they end up <u>happily married</u> with children.

3) Compeyson ends up <u>drowned</u> in the Thames — Jack searches for his body to <u>steal his stockings</u>.

4) Drummle <u>abuses</u> Estella. He is <u>killed</u> by a horse that he <u>mistreats</u>.

Crime and Justice

Crime and justice are themes that keep popping up all the way through the novel. Almost everywhere Pip turns he runs into criminals or symbols of crime. He doesn't like it much, but then again, neither would you...

Most characters feel guilty for doing bad things

Most characters in *Great Expectations* feel guilty for things they've done, even if they haven't broken the law.

1) Miss Havisham deliberately makes Pip miserable by encouraging him to love Estella, and she teaches Estella never to love anyone. Near the end of the book she admits her guilt, repeating, "What have I done!"

2) At the end of the novel Estella asks for Pip's forgiveness — she's realised what she threw away when she rejected him and feels guilty about treating him badly.

3) Dickens shows his characters feeling guilty so you feel sympathy for them — they're sorry for what they've done so they deserve to be forgiven.

> Not all characters feel guilty though. Compeyson destroys Miss Havisham's life and Drummle mistreats Estella once they're married. You don't hear anything about them regretting what they've done, but they do get what's coming to them. See p.46.

4) Dickens also questions whether some crimes are justified. Pip and Herbert break the law when they try to help Magwitch escape, and Magwitch kills Compeyson, but you get the sense that this is just (fair) even though they're not being punished within the legal system.

© Robert Brookes

Most of the characters are forgiven

In *Great Expectations* the characters who feel guilty about their actions make up for them.

1) Pip makes up for rejecting Magwitch and for his bad treatment of Joe by looking after Magwitch when he's dying and asking Joe to forgive him.

2) Estella learns to appreciate Pip's love during her abusive marriage to Drummle. She begs him to forgive her for the way she's treated him — they finish the novel as friends.

3) Miss Havisham apologises for what she's done to Pip and tries to make it up to him by giving him the money for Herbert's job. She tries to put right what she's done, but she still dies after the fire in her house. However, this could be because locking herself away from the world has led to her having a "profound unfitness for this earth" — it's as if she gave up on her life years ago and death is a release.

Dickens believed that novels should encourage people to act in the right way. One of the messages in *Great Expectations* is that even after doing something wrong, you can still be forgiven and have a happy future if you try to put things right.

Revise a few key examples for each theme...

There's lots to take in here but don't worry — you don't have to remember it word for word. Memorise the main headings, then a couple of examples for each one. That way you'll be well prepared for your exam.

Relationships

Breaking news — *Great Expectations* isn't all doom and gloom. There are loads of different relationships to talk about as well. Love's a really important part of *Great Expectations,* although it's not exactly a rom com.

Characters who give love find love

One of the major <u>messages</u> of *Great Expectations* is that <u>relationships</u> are the most <u>important</u> thing in life. <u>Some</u> characters know this from the beginning and Dickens <u>rewards</u> them for it by giving them <u>happy lives</u>.

1) Joe <u>loves</u> Pip even though they're not <u>related</u>. Biddy loves and <u>cares for</u> Pip even when he <u>hardly notices</u> her. Biddy and Joe eventually get married and live a <u>happy contented life</u>.

2) Herbert marries Clara even though his family think she's <u>not good enough</u> for him and they build a happy life together.

3) Wemmick treats his father (the Aged P) with <u>huge affection</u> and is a <u>loyal</u> friend to Pip. He ends up <u>happily married</u> to Miss Skiffins.

Some characters seem unable to love

1) Some characters in the novel don't seem to be able to <u>love anyone</u>. Mrs Joe <u>beats</u> Pip and Joe, and isn't ever <u>kind</u> to either of them. Estella's been trained to <u>bury her feelings</u> — she tells Pip she has "<u>no heart</u>". Miss Havisham <u>flatters</u> and <u>praises</u> Estella, but doesn't show her much <u>love</u>.

2) All of these characters have <u>bad relationships</u> — Mrs Joe is <u>attacked</u>, Estella is <u>physically abused</u> by Drummle and Miss Havisham is <u>rejected</u> by Estella. This makes them realise how valuable <u>loving relationships</u> are. As a result, Mrs Joe's "<u>temper</u> was greatly improved", Estella <u>regrets</u> throwing away Pip's love when she was "ignorant of its worth" and Miss Havisham <u>begs</u> Pip for <u>forgiveness</u>.

3) A lot of the characters who can't love are <u>women</u> — Dickens doesn't portray women particularly <u>sympathetically</u>.

Pip's loyal to Estella

Pip's relationship with <u>Estella</u> is really <u>important</u>.

1) It's the reason he <u>first</u> starts to think that he isn't <u>good enough</u>. It's her comments about his "coarse hands" and "thick boots" that make him <u>ambitious</u> and obsessed with <u>social class</u>.

2) It stops him from realising that Biddy loves him and that they'd probably be <u>happy</u> together if they married.

3) His <u>loyalty</u> pays off when they become <u>friends</u> — although the reader is left <u>wondering</u> what happens to them in the end.

© Moviestore Collection Ltd

Relationships

Now that love's all over and done with it's time to talk about friendship. Friends in *Great Expectations* help each other with money, do favours for each other, and save each other's lives. I wish I had some friends *sob*.

Pip has two important friends

1) Pip's first real friend is Joe — he's like a father to him. When Pip becomes a gentleman he feels awkward about his lower-class past, and avoids seeing Joe — but Joe stays loyal to Pip.

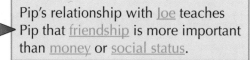

Pip's relationship with Joe teaches Pip that friendship is more important than money or social status.

2) Pip and Herbert fight the first time they meet at Satis House, but soon make friends when they meet again in London. Pip ends up working for Herbert in Egypt to pay off his debts.

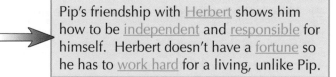

Pip's friendship with Herbert shows him how to be independent and responsible for himself. Herbert doesn't have a fortune so he has to work hard for a living, unlike Pip.

Pip has several father figures

The novel is all about Pip growing up and becoming a better person. Dickens gives him father figures to help.

1) Pip's relationships with Joe and Magwitch teach him that friendship and loyalty are more important than social class.

2) Pip's ashamed of Joe, but Joe comes to care for him when he's ill and pays off all of his debts even though he's just a poor blacksmith.

3) But Magwitch isn't always a good father figure. He forces Pip to steal from Joe and Mrs Joe and what he does for Pip is largely motivated by a desire to get revenge on society.

© ITV/Rex Features

Character — Miss Havisham

Miss Havisham isn't a good mother figure either. She exploits Estella to get her own revenge on men.

Pip has to learn what true love and friendship are

1) Young, immature Pip values money, class and nice clothes, and only really cares what rich posh people like Estella and Miss Havisham think about him. The older, more mature Pip realises that other things are more important: kindness, taking care of others, and loyalty to your friends.

Pip learns what's important in life when Magwitch is dying in prison after the escape attempt. Magwitch supported him for years even though he hardly knew who Pip was and risked death to see Pip again.

2) Pip repays Herbert for his friendship by getting him a job. At the end of the book, he also repays the love and loyalty he has had from Joe and Biddy by visiting them and begging them to forgive him.

KEY QUOTE

"Tell me of my ingratitude. Don't be so good to me!"

Joe's such a good friend to Pip that Pip almost can't bear it — he feels guilty for having treated Joe so badly, when Joe has only ever been lovely to him. He's finally realised what a snob he was... and about time too.

Practice Questions

There's a pretty good chance you'll get questions about themes in the exam so use these questions to check you've understood the hairy blighters. Go on — they're only short little ones...

Quick Questions

1) Name one 'bad' upper class character in *Great Expectations*.

2) How is Pip treated differently at the Blue Boar inn when he's poor?

3) Give two examples of ambitious characters in the novel.

4) Name two characters who use Pip to get what they want.

5) Give two symbols of crime in the novel.

6) Give one example of Jaggers bending the law to help someone.

7) Give an example of a character who gets what they deserve.

8) Which three characters in *Great Expectations* seem unable to love anyone?

9) Which of Pip's friends teaches him the value of working hard for a living?

10) Name two characters who could be seen as father figures to Pip.

Practice Questions

You've done your warm-up — all your brain cells should be limbered up and raring to go. Give them a full workout with these in-depth and exam-style questions. Take your time and read the questions thoroughly.

In-depth Questions

1) Do you think Dickens portrays ambition in a positive way? Why / Why not?

2) Write a paragraph explaining how education is both positive and negative in the novel.

3) Does Miss Havisham deserve to die at the end of the novel? Explain your answer.

4) Do you think Dickens portrays love in a positive way? Why / Why not?

5) Which character do you think teaches Pip the most in *Great Expectations*? What does he / she teach him?

Exam-style Questions

1) How does Pip's awareness of social class affect his relationships in *Great Expectations*?

2) How does Dickens present the theme of ambition in *Great Expectations*?

3) How does Dickens use *Great Expectations* to explore ideas about crime and justice?

4) How is love presented as sometimes positive and sometimes negative in different parts of the novel?

5) a) Explain how Dickens shows the significance of Pip's relationship with Magwitch in Chapter 56.

   b) Explain Pip's attitude to Magwitch in another part of the novel, using examples of Dickens' language to back up your answer.

Form and Structure

Quite a lot of people think Charles Dickens had the writing X factor. Whether you agree or whether you think it's all just a lot of hype, this section's here to explain what exactly Dickens is supposed to be so good at.

'Great Expectations' was published as a serial

1) In the <u>nineteenth century</u> buying books was really expensive so many novels were published in <u>serial form</u>. The publishers released a <u>few chapters</u> at a time in <u>magazines</u> that came out every week or month.

2) Each instalment had to be as <u>interesting</u> or as <u>exciting</u> as the last one. That's why something <u>important</u> happens every few pages in *Great Expectations*. To make people buy the <u>next instalment</u>, writers like Dickens often included <u>cliffhangers</u> at the end of a section.

> There's one at the end of Chapter Four, when it seems Pip's about to be <u>arrested</u>, and another at the end of Chapter 44 when Pip gets the <u>mysterious note</u> saying "DON'T GO HOME."

© Moviestore Collection Ltd

The novel is a bildungsroman

1) A <u>bildungsroman</u> is a story where the <u>main character</u> grows from a <u>child</u> into an <u>adult</u> and <u>learns</u> a lot about himself / herself along the way.

2) *Great Expectations* has lots of the <u>features</u> that are typical of this kind of novel:

- The hero <u>gradually grows</u> from a boy into a man.
- He has <u>setbacks</u> along the way.
- <u>Money</u> is a big part of his ambitions.
- The <u>ending</u> isn't very <u>clear</u>.
- The story is partly <u>autobiographical</u>.

Pip's life in 'Great Expectations' is partly based on Dickens' own life. As a child he was forced to work to pay off his father's debts and he also rose from his poor background to be a very rich man.

Dickens uses satire a lot in 'Great Expectations'

Dickens uses <u>humour</u> to poke <u>fun</u> at the <u>society</u> he lives in — this is called <u>satire</u>. For example:

1) He criticises the <u>education system</u> at the time by <u>making fun</u> of Mr Wopsle's great-aunt's <u>school</u>.

2) He makes fun of people who are obsessed with <u>class</u> and climbing the <u>social scale</u> by writing about <u>ridiculous characters</u> like Uncle Pumblechook, Mr Wopsle and Mrs Pocket.

3) He criticises the <u>legal system</u> by showing how Jaggers reacts to the <u>false witness</u> in Chapter 20.

Write about how Dickens creates tension...

Dickens' readers had to wait for each new instalment of *Great Expectations*, so all these cliffhangers had people on the edge of their seats. You could mention how the cliffhangers create dramatic tension for us, too.

How Characters Speak

Dickens deliberately chose the words he put in his characters' mouths. It's not just what they say but how they say it — look at their accents, catchphrases and how posh they sound. This'll tell you about their class.

Accent reveals a character's class

Dickens writes some of the <u>words</u> the way the lower-class characters would have <u>pronounced</u> them:

- <u>Magwitch</u> says "wittles" not 'victuals'.

- <u>Joe</u> says "chawed" for 'chewed', "elth" for 'health' and "conwict" for 'convict'.

1) <u>Joe</u> and <u>Magwitch's</u> language is the most different from standard English because they're from the <u>lowest social class</u>.

2) <u>Middle</u> and <u>upper class</u> characters like the Pockets and Miss Havisham all use <u>standard English</u>.

3) When Pip first goes to Satis House Dickens deliberately brings out the <u>contrast</u> between <u>Pip's</u> way of speaking and <u>Estella's</u>. She teases Pip for using different words — "He calls the knaves, Jacks, this boy!" This <u>emphasises</u> the difference between their <u>social classes</u>.

4) As he gets older, Pip <u>learns</u> to speak like a <u>middle class</u> young man. Speaking the right way was an important part of being a <u>gentleman</u> at the time.

Theme — Social Class

Some <u>upper class</u> people in *Great Expectations* say things just because society <u>expects</u> them to, even when they're clearly <u>ridiculous</u> — for example Sarah Pocket tells Miss Havisham "How <u>well</u> you look!" even though she looks <u>terrible</u>.

Dickens uses characters' language to reveal their personalities

Dickens doesn't just use his characters' <u>language</u> to tell you about their <u>class</u> — he also uses it to tell you about their <u>personality</u> or their <u>feelings</u>. Some <u>phrases</u> and ways of <u>speaking</u> make his characters really <u>memorable</u>.

1) Jaggers always talks in <u>semi-official</u> language, showing how his whole life is focussed on his work as a <u>lawyer</u>.

2) Joe's very <u>comfortable</u> when he's in the <u>forge</u> but he <u>tangles</u> his words when he's visiting Miss Havisham at <u>Satis House</u> — "and by them which your liberal present—have—conweyed —to be—for the satisfaction of mind—of—them as never—".

3) When Joe <u>visits Pip</u> in London for the first time, he <u>stops</u> calling him "<u>old chap</u>" and calls him "<u>sir</u>" instead. Now Pip's a <u>gentleman</u>, Joe doesn't feel that he's <u>good enough</u> to talk to him like an <u>equal</u>.

4) Mrs Joe's language <u>changes</u> when she's trying to <u>impress</u> people. Usually she <u>makes up</u> her own words and expressions like "Pompeyed" but when Uncle Pumblechook visits at Christmas she says "you must taste, to finish with, such a delightful and delicious present of Uncle Pumblechook's!"

© Moviestore Collection Ltd

"He calls the knaves, Jacks, this boy!"

You can open *Great Expectations* nearly anywhere and find somebody gassing away in their own particular style and accent. Dickens doesn't just turn up the language dial occasionally — it's on high at all times.

Point of View and Narrative

Every story — from *Spot Goes to School* to *The Iliad* — has a point of view. In *Great Expectations* the story's told from Pip's point of view. We see what he sees, feel what he feels, eat what he eats... No, wait, hang on...

The story is told by Pip looking back on his life

© Robert Brookes

1) The story is told in Pip's <u>voice</u> — he's a <u>first-person narrator</u> (he says '<u>I</u> went to London' not '<u>he</u> went to London').

2) Pip's writing <u>some time</u> after his final meeting with Estella at Satis House. It's the <u>older</u>, <u>wiser</u>, <u>more grown-up</u> Pip who's telling the story, so he's able to <u>comment</u> when his <u>younger</u> self does something <u>stupid</u> or <u>selfish</u>.

3) Pip tells you what he saw and did <u>as he remembers it</u> years later, so you get his <u>opinion</u>, not a <u>balanced</u> view.

4) The fact that the narrator Pip is <u>kinder</u> and more <u>humble</u> shows that, even though younger Pip can be <u>selfish</u> and <u>arrogant</u> in the novel, he must turn out <u>okay</u> in the end and <u>become</u> the wise narrator-Pip.

Pip plays on your emotions

1) Pip appeals to the reader's <u>emotions</u>. He introduces himself as a <u>little orphaned boy</u> who's so young he can't even say his own <u>name</u> properly, even though he's much <u>older</u> when he's <u>writing</u>.

2) As a <u>first-person narrator</u>, Pip can describe exactly what he's <u>feeling</u> at the time. This helps the reader <u>relate</u> to Pip — you can really <u>imagine</u> what he's going through so it's easier to feel <u>sympathy</u> for him.

3) For example, when Estella tells him she's going to <u>marry Drummle</u>, he feels "<u>agony</u>" and his speech about how much he loves her is like "<u>blood</u> from an <u>inward wound</u>". This shows just how <u>devastated</u> he is.

The novel looks back to an earlier age

The story starts some time between <u>1800</u> and <u>1820</u>, but Dickens was writing in the <u>1860s</u>. This means that Pip grows up during the <u>same period</u> that <u>Dickens</u> and many of his <u>readers</u> grew up. This would have helped his readers <u>relate</u> to Pip and <u>imagine</u> his life. There are lots of <u>details</u> that help with this.

1) In the <u>1860s</u>, somebody travelling from Kent to London would take the <u>train</u>, but Pip travels by <u>stagecoach</u> and stays at <u>coaching inns</u>.

2) <u>Photography</u> wasn't invented until the 1830s, so Pip doesn't know what his parents <u>looked like</u> — "their days were <u>long before</u> the days of photographs."

Mention why Dickens uses the first person...

This stuff isn't easy. You've got to know that Pip is a first-person narrator, but you also need to say what effect this has on the novel... If you can't, then try having another little look at this page before moving on.

Doubles

One of Dickens' weirder tricks in *Great Expectations* is the way he uses 'doubles'. Many characters, events and settings have mirror images. Here are a few examples, but there are loads more if you look for them.

Some of the characters are doubles

Some of the <u>characters</u> in *Great Expectations* are <u>doubles</u> of each other — they're <u>similar</u> to each other in some way. <u>Comparing</u> these pairs of characters helps Dickens to put across his <u>message</u>.

Miss Havisham and Magwitch

- Miss Havisham and Magwitch both 'adopt' <u>orphans</u> (Estella and Pip) and give them <u>fortunes</u>.

- They're both very <u>obsessed</u> — Miss Havisham devotes her <u>whole life</u> to making Estella cruel and cold. Magwitch <u>risks</u> his <u>life</u> to go back to England and see Pip as a gentleman.

- Dickens uses these characters to show how <u>destructive</u> it can be to follow <u>obsessive dreams</u>.

Pip and Herbert

- <u>Herbert</u> is about the <u>same age</u> as Pip. He's trying to <u>make his way</u> in the big city and is <u>in love</u> with a girl he hopes to marry, just like Pip. He represents Pip's <u>good side</u>.

Pip and Drummle

- <u>Drummle</u> represents Pip's <u>bad side</u>. He has what Pip <u>wants</u> — titles, money, class and Estella, but he's <u>selfish</u> and <u>snobby</u>. He brings out the <u>worst</u> in Pip. Dickens is <u>hinting</u> that Pip has the <u>wrong dreams</u> — these things won't make him <u>happy</u>.

Joe and Magwitch

- Joe and Magwitch are both <u>father-figures</u> to Pip (see p.49). They're from <u>poor</u>, lower class backgrounds, have little <u>education</u> and are <u>kind</u> to Pip. He <u>rejects</u> them both but later he realises how <u>ungrateful</u> he's been.

- By <u>comparing</u> Magwitch to Joe, Dickens shows that he's a <u>good person</u>, just like Joe.

Photo: akg-images / album / Rank

Some situations in the novel are repeated

1) There are <u>parallels</u> between the first and second times <u>Magwitch</u> appears. At both meetings Pip thinks Magwitch eats like a <u>dog</u>. When they first meet, Magwitch is dressed in <u>grey</u> and his leg is clamped in <u>iron</u>. Later on, his hair is "<u>iron grey</u>".

2) This helps the reader compare Pip's <u>reaction</u> to Magwitch in the two meetings. In the first one, he's really <u>scared</u> of Magwitch, but in the second he's just <u>disgusted</u> by him because Magwitch is so far below Pip's <u>social class</u> — he's become a <u>snob</u>.

Writer's Techniques — Narrators

Dickens also uses a '<u>double narrator</u>' in *Great Expectations*. Pip tells <u>most</u> of the story as if he was the <u>age</u> he is in the <u>story</u>, but sometimes he makes <u>comments</u> as Pip writing when he's much <u>older</u>. This means Dickens can give the reader <u>clues</u> about what's <u>going</u> to happen. For example, after his first visit to <u>Satis House</u> he says "it made <u>great changes</u> in me" but he couldn't have <u>known</u> this at the <u>time</u>.

KEY QUOTE

"and there... looking at the fire, was — I again!"

Here's another double in the novel — when Pip returns to the forge, he meets Joe's son, young Pip. Young Pip shows that our Pip has become a better person — Joe hopes his son will "grow a little bit like" Pip.

Settings

Setting is really important in *Great Expectations*. Dickens uses descriptions of setting to add atmosphere. Imagine if London had been all bright lights and marble hallways — it would've been a very different story...

London is gloomy and menacing

1) When Pip first arrives in London he thinks it's "ugly, crooked, narrow, and dirty". <u>Smithfield</u> meat market is "all asmear with filth and fat and blood and foam" and in <u>Newgate Prison</u> he's shown a <u>gallows</u> and the place where people are "publicly whipped".

2) London seems <u>dirty</u> and full of <u>corruption</u>. This suggests that it won't be the place where Pip's <u>dreams</u> of becoming a gentleman come true. Instead, he'll be <u>corrupted</u> by his <u>money</u> and his new life in the city.

© ITV/Rex Features

The forge starts scary but ends up happy

1) Although Dickens disliked the <u>city</u>, he doesn't <u>pretend</u> that the countryside is <u>perfect</u>. The marshes are scary and the living conditions aren't very healthy — Pip's five brothers have all died.

2) While <u>Mrs Joe</u> is alive the forge is often a <u>scary</u> place. She keeps "Tickler" on permanent display and Pip has to go to bed in the <u>dark</u> — Mrs Joe won't let him take a candle up to bed.

3) When <u>Biddy</u> and Joe are <u>married</u> everything <u>changes</u>. In the sitting room, "the carpet had been taken away, and the room kept always fresh and wholesome night and day".

Satis House is a spooky setting

1) The house is large and packed with expensive furniture but it's all <u>crumbling</u>. This suggests that <u>money</u> and <u>possessions</u> are not <u>enough</u> to make you <u>happy</u> and won't last forever.

2) The disused brewery shows that the place was once <u>productive</u> and full of life. Now it's empty and <u>abandoned</u>. Even the animals have left — "there were no pigeons in the dove-cot, no horses in the stable, no pigs in the sty". <u>Nothing</u> can live there, everything just <u>rots</u>.

3) The <u>stopped clocks</u> show how Miss Havisham is <u>stuck in the past</u>, obsessed with the moment when she was jilted. Pip's <u>visits</u> to the house all seem to be very <u>similar</u>, adding to the feeling that <u>nothing</u> in the house ever <u>changes</u>.

4) Satis House is <u>completely dark</u> — "No glimpse of daylight was to be seen" in Miss Havisham's room. This gives the reader a sense that there are <u>secrets</u> in the house (Miss Havisham's story is a secret for a long time) and that Miss Havisham shouldn't be <u>trusted</u> because Pip can't <u>see clearly</u>.

KEY QUOTE

"This is a pretty pleasure-ground, sir."

Wemmick's house really stands out in *Great Expectations*, partly because most of the other settings are so depressing. It might not be an actual castle, but it's got such a happy vibe — beats dirty old Smithfield...

Symbolism and Imagery

Dickens uses lots of interesting symbols in *Great Expectations*. There are too many to squeeze onto just one page, but here are some to get you started. Jot down any others you notice while you're reading the book.

Mist can mean different things in the novel

1) When Pip takes food to Magwitch he feels the <u>mist</u> is coming to <u>get him</u> — "The mist was <u>heavier yet</u> when I got out upon the marshes, so that instead of my running at everything, everything seemed to <u>run at me</u>." The mist <u>symbolises</u> his <u>confusion</u> and <u>fear</u> — he thinks the <u>convict</u> is going to <u>get him</u> too.

2) When Pip's travelling to <u>London</u> for the first time the mists have "<u>solemnly risen</u>" and Pip feels like "the world lay <u>spread before me</u>." His <u>dreams</u> have come true and he's full of <u>hope</u> about his new life.

3) At the <u>end</u> of the novel, as Pip and Estella walk off holding hands, the <u>mists rise</u> again, just like they rose "long ago when I first left the forge". Dickens could be saying that Pip's about to start a new and <u>happy life</u> with Estella, or this might mean that it won't be as <u>amazing</u> as Pip imagines — just like <u>London</u>.

Dickens uses weather and lighting to change the mood

© ITV/Rex Features

1) In *Great Expectations*, <u>darkness</u> and <u>bad weather</u> suggest that bad things are about to happen. <u>Bright light</u> suggests that things are <u>looking up</u>.

2) After Mrs Joe's funeral, <u>Joe</u> works in the forge with a "<u>glow</u> of health and strength" on his face. Pip thinks it's the "<u>bright sun</u>" of Joe's new life <u>shining</u> onto him. <u>Light</u> symbolises that life without Mrs Joe will be more hopeful.

3) When Orlick <u>traps</u> Pip in the sluice-house he shuts out the <u>light</u> and lights a candle instead. It seems as if Pip's <u>hope</u> of surviving has <u>gone</u> with the <u>light</u>.

4) The <u>weather</u> on the day of Magwitch's <u>escape</u> attempt is <u>bright</u>, <u>clear</u> and <u>sunny</u>. But during the <u>night</u>, the <u>wind</u> picks up and it becomes really <u>cold</u>. From this point everything goes <u>wrong</u>.

Dickens uses imagery to describe his characters

1) <u>Miss Havisham</u> is surrounded by images of <u>death</u>. At their first meeting, Pip describes her as "<u>withered</u>" and with "<u>sunken eyes</u>", just like a dead body. She's <u>given up</u> on life and locked herself away to <u>rot</u>.

2) Estella's name means 'star' and Pip describes the way she carries a <u>light</u> along the dark hallways of Satis House "like a <u>star</u>". This gives the impression that, like a star, Estella is <u>beautiful</u>, but also <u>inaccessible</u> to him. Pip also says that her face is "like a <u>statue's</u>" — this makes her seem <u>cold</u> and <u>unfeeling</u>.

Write about a variety of different symbols and images...

Well, that's your lot for symbols and images. There are lots more in the book though, so if you find other examples in the novel, and you can back up your ideas with evidence, include them in your revision.

Descriptions and Comparisons

If Dickens' descriptions were hamburgers they would be quarter pounders with bacon, double cheese, mayo, lettuce and a few tomatoes. He really likes to lay it on thick. With a shovel. And sometimes a dumper truck.

Dickens' descriptions help readers experience the story

Dickens doesn't just say <u>what things look like</u>. He also uses description to <u>set the mood</u>. Sometimes this is really <u>blatant</u> — like a storm before something bad happens. Sometimes it's more <u>subtle</u>.

Barnard's Inn is ugly and disappointing

- Dickens <u>repeats</u> words to <u>emphasise</u> how awful Pip's first impression of Barnard's Inn is — "it had the most <u>dismal</u> trees in it, and the most <u>dismal</u> sparrows, and the most <u>dismal</u> cats, and the most <u>dismal</u> houses".

- He also uses alliteration — "<u>d</u>usty <u>d</u>ecay, and <u>m</u>iserable <u>m</u>akeshift". This description shows just how <u>disappointed</u> Pip is with his new life.

The brewery at Satis House is a moody backdrop

- Dickens describes the brewery using <u>different senses</u>.

- He writes about the <u>temperature</u> — "The <u>cold</u> wind seemed to blow <u>colder</u> there than outside the gate".

- He also tells you how things <u>sound</u>. He says the cold wind, "made a <u>shrill noise</u> in <u>howling</u> in and out at the open sides of the brewery" and was "like the noise of <u>wind</u> in the rigging of a ship at sea". This makes it seem <u>unfriendly</u> and emphasises the fact that it's <u>run-down</u> and <u>empty</u>.

© ITV/Rex Features

Dickens references other well-known stories

Dickens uses <u>images</u> from stories in the <u>Bible</u> or <u>Shakespeare</u> plays to make his writing more <u>interesting</u>. Most middle-class readers in the <u>1860s</u> would have read Shakespeare, and would know the Bible very well, so these <u>comparisons</u> would help them <u>understand</u> what Dickens was trying to say.

1) After Pip sees <u>Mr Wopsle's</u> acting, he dreams about playing <u>Hamlet</u> himself. <u>Pip's</u> a bit like Hamlet, because he's searching for his <u>identity</u> and sees <u>visions</u>.

2) Pip's vision of the <u>file</u> in <u>Chapter Ten</u> is like Macbeth's vision of a <u>dagger</u> just before he stabs Duncan. This <u>comparison</u> shows that Pip feels really <u>guilty</u> — just like Macbeth. He's also comparing <u>stealing</u> a file with <u>murder</u>.

3) The way Jaggers is always washing his hands would have reminded Dickens' readers of <u>Lady Macbeth's guilt</u> (she feels as if she <u>can't</u> wash the <u>blood</u> off her <u>hands</u>) and suggests that <u>Jaggers</u> feels <u>guilty</u> too.

4) Jaggers is also like <u>Pontius Pilate</u>, who washed his hands before <u>Jesus's crucifixion</u> to show that he wouldn't take <u>responsibility</u> for it — just like <u>Jaggers</u> doesn't take responsibility for his <u>clients</u>.

Make your exams easier by practising your answers...

So there you have it. There's a load of new info in this section, and it'll all be useful in your exam. The best way to remember it all? Some practice questions, I reckon — there's some lying in wait over the page...

Practice Questions

Wouldn't it be magical if there was a way for you to make sure you've got the hang of the stuff in this section. Maybe about ten quick-fire questions... Sadly we don't have the technology. It just can't be done...

Quick Questions

1) How many volumes are there in *Great Expectations*?

2) Write down two features of *Great Expectations* that make it a 'bildungsroman'.

3) What does the way Joe speaks tell you about his character?

4) What is a first-person narrator?

5) *Great Expectations* is set quite a long time before Dickens wrote it. Give one detail from the novel which shows this.

6) Name two characters who could be described as Pip's doubles.

7) Why could Magwitch and Miss Havisham be seen as doubles?

8) Everything in Satis House is crumbling. What does this tell you about money and possessions?

9) After Mrs Joe's funeral, what does the glow on Joe's face symbolise?

10) Give two reasons why Pip is a bit like Hamlet.

Practice Questions

Now for some hard-core questions. Pens and paper at the ready, please. The exam-style questions are great to do as part of your revision — answering them is a cracking way to practise your essay-writing technique.

In-depth Questions

1) Write a paragraph explaining how you can tell that *Great Expectations* was written as a serial.

2) Explain how Dickens makes it clear that his lower class characters speak with an accent.

3) Why is it useful to have the novel narrated by an older, more mature Pip?

4) Find an event in the novel which happens twice and explain why you think Dickens 'doubled' it in this way.

5) Explain how the way Dickens describes Satis House adds to the overall mood of the novel.

Exam-style Questions

1) Choose one character from the novel. Show how Dickens uses their speech to bring out their personality.

2) How does Dickens use 'doubles' to show how his characters' reactions to events change over the course of the novel?

3) How does Dickens use satire to comment on society at the time when he was writing?

4) What does the first-person narration in *Great Expectations* contribute to the novel?

5) Show how Dickens uses description to create tension in two different chapters of *Great Expectations*.

Exam Preparation

Getting to know the text will put you at a massive advantage in the exam. It's not enough just to read it though — you've got to get to grips with the nitty-gritty bits. It's all about gathering evidence...

The exam questions will test four main skills

You will need to show the examiner that you can:

1) Write about the text in a thoughtful way — picking out appropriate examples and quotations to back up your opinions.

2) Identify and explain features of the text's form, structure and language. Show how the author uses these to create meanings and effects.

> Not all exam boards will test you on this. Check with your teacher.

3) Relate the text to its cultural, social and historical background (e.g. Britain in the 1800s).

4) Write in a clear, well-structured way. 5% of the marks in your English Literature exams are for spelling, punctuation and grammar. Make sure that your writing is as accurate as possible.

Preparation is important

1) It's important to cover all the different sections of this book in your revision. You need to make sure you understand the text's context, plot, characters, themes and writer's techniques.

2) In the exam, you'll need to bring together your ideas about these topics to answer the question quickly.

3) Think about the different characters and themes in the text, and write down some key points and ideas about each one. Then, find some evidence to support each point — this could be something from any of the sections in this book. You could set out your evidence in a table like this:

Theme: Ambition	
Pip's ambition	Pip is born into a working class family but wants to be a gentleman — "I wished I was not common".
Education	Pip asks Biddy for lessons so he can be a gentleman. Mrs Joe doesn't want Joe to be educated — he might "rise".
Happiness	Ambition isn't what makes you happy — Joe doesn't have big ambitions and is the happiest character.
Working hard	If you work hard at your ambition then it's not a bad thing, e.g. Herbert Pocket, Wemmick's castle.
Selfishness	Ambitious characters like Pumblechook and the Pockets use others to get ahead. Pip neglects his family.

Preparing to succeed — a cunning plot indeed...

Knowing the plot inside out will be unbelievably helpful in the exam. It'll help you to stay calm and make sure you write a brilliant answer that positively glitters with little gems of evidence. The exam's just a chance for you to show off...

The Exam Question

This page deals with how to approach an exam question. The stuff below will help you get started on a scorching exam answer, more scorching than, say, a phoenix cooking fiery fajitas in a flaming furnace.

Read the question carefully and underline key words

Henry didn't read the weather report carefully enough when planning his weekend activities.

1) The style of question you'll get depends on which <u>exam board</u> you're taking.

2) Read all the <u>instructions</u> carefully. Make sure you know <u>how many</u> questions you need to answer and <u>how much time</u> you should spend answering each one.

3) If the question has <u>more than one part</u>, look at the total number of marks for each bit. This should help you to plan your <u>time</u> in the exam.

4) <u>Read</u> the question at least <u>twice</u> so you completely understand it. <u>Underline</u> the key words. If you're given an <u>extract</u>, underline <u>important</u> words or phrases in that too.

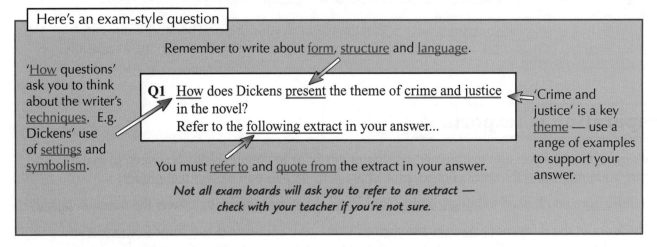

Here's an exam-style question

Remember to write about <u>form</u>, <u>structure</u> and <u>language</u>.

'<u>How</u> questions' ask you to think about the writer's <u>techniques</u>. E.g. Dickens' use of <u>settings</u> and <u>symbolism</u>.

Q1 <u>How</u> does Dickens <u>present</u> the theme of <u>crime and justice</u> in the novel?
Refer to the <u>following extract</u> in your answer...

'Crime and justice' is a key <u>theme</u> — use a range of examples to support your answer.

You must <u>refer to</u> and <u>quote from</u> the extract in your answer.

Not all exam boards will ask you to refer to an extract — check with your teacher if you're not sure.

Get to know exam language

Some <u>words</u> come up time and again in <u>exam questions</u>. Have a look at some <u>specimen</u> questions, pick out words that are <u>often used</u> in questions and make sure that you <u>understand</u> what they mean. You could <u>write a few down</u> whilst you're revising. For example:

Question Word	You need to...
Explore / Explain	Show <u>how</u> the writer deals with a <u>theme</u>, <u>character</u> or <u>idea</u>. Make several <u>different</u> points to answer the question.
How does	Think about the <u>techniques</u> or <u>literary features</u> that the author uses to get their point across.
Give examples	Use <u>direct quotes</u> and describe <u>events</u> from the text in your own words.
Refer to	Read the question so that you know if you need to write about just an <u>extract</u>, or an extract and the <u>rest of the text</u>.

The advice squad — the best cops in the NYPD...

Whatever question you're asked in the exam, your answer should touch on the main characters, themes, structure and language of the text. All the stuff we've covered in the rest of the book in fact. It's so neat, it's almost like we planned it.

Planning Your Answer

I'll say this once — and then I'll probably repeat it several times — it is absolutely, completely, totally and utterly essential that you make a plan before you start writing. Only a fool jumps right in without a plan...

Plan your answer before you start

1) If you plan, you're less likely to forget something <u>important</u>.

2) A good plan will help you <u>organise</u> your ideas — and write a good, <u>well-structured</u> essay.

3) Write your plan at the <u>top of your answer booklet</u> and draw a <u>neat line</u> through it when you've finished.

4) <u>Don't</u> spend <u>too long</u> on your plan. It's only <u>rough work</u>, so you don't need to write in full sentences. Here are a few <u>examples</u> of different ways you can plan your answer:

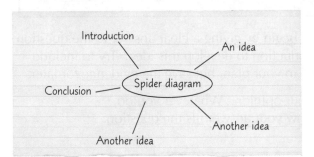

Bullet points...

- Introduction...
- An idea...
- The next idea...
- Another idea...
- Yet another idea...
- Conclusion...

Include bits of evidence in your plan

1) <u>Writing</u> your essay will be much <u>easier</u> if you include <u>important quotes</u> and <u>examples</u> in your plan.

2) You could include them in a <u>table</u> like this one:

3) <u>Don't</u> spend <u>too long</u> writing out quotes though. It's just to make sure you <u>don't forget</u> anything when you write your answer.

A point...	Quote to back this up...
Another point...	Quote...
A different point...	Example...
A brand new point...	Quote...

Structure your answer

Introduction
↓
Middle Section
— paragraphs
expanding
your
argument.
↓
Conclusion

1) Your <u>introduction</u> should give a brief answer to the question you're writing about. Make it clear how you're going to <u>tackle the topic</u>.

2) The <u>middle section</u> of your essay should explain your answer in detail and give evidence to back it up. Write a <u>paragraph</u> for each point you make. Make sure you <u>comment</u> on your evidence and <u>explain how</u> it helps to <u>prove</u> your point.

3) Remember to write a <u>conclusion</u> — a paragraph at the end which <u>sums up</u> your <u>main points</u>. There's <u>more</u> about introductions and conclusions on the <u>next page</u>.

Dirk finally felt ready
to tackle the topic.

To plan or not to plan, that is the question...

The answer is yes, yes, a thousand times yes. Often students dive right in, worried that planning will take up valuable time. But 5 minutes spent organising a well-structured answer is loads better than pages of waffle. Mmm waffles.

Writing Introductions and Conclusions

Now you've made that plan that I was banging on about on the last page, you'll know what your main points are. This is going to make writing your introduction and conclusion as easy as pie.

Get to the point straight away in your introduction

1) First, you need to <u>work out</u> what the question is <u>asking you</u> to do:

> How is the character of Joe important to the novel?

> The question is <u>asking you</u> to think about the <u>role</u> of <u>Joe</u> in the text.
> Plan your essay by thinking about <u>how</u> this character <u>links</u> to the text's overall <u>message</u>.

2) When you've <u>planned</u> your essay, you should <u>begin</u> by giving a <u>clear answer</u> to the <u>question</u> in a sentence or two. Use the <u>rest</u> of the <u>introduction</u> to <u>develop</u> this idea. Try to include the <u>main paragraph ideas</u> that you have listed in your plan, but <u>save</u> the <u>evidence</u> for later.

3) You could also use the <u>introduction</u> to give your <u>opinion</u>. Whatever you do, make sure your introduction makes it <u>clear</u> how your answer <u>fits the question</u>.

Your conclusion must answer the question

1) The <u>most important</u> thing you have to do at the <u>end</u> of your writing is to <u>summarise</u> your <u>answer</u> to the question.

2) It's your <u>last chance</u> to persuade the examiner, so make your <u>main point</u> again.

3) Use your <u>last sentence</u> to really <u>impress</u> the <u>examiner</u> — it will make your essay <u>stand out</u>. You could <u>develop</u> your own <u>opinion</u> of the text or <u>highlight</u> which of your <u>points</u> you thought was the most <u>interesting</u>.

The examiner was struggling to see the answer clearly.

Use the question words in your introduction and conclusion

1) Try to use <u>words</u> or <u>phrases</u> from the <u>question</u> in your introduction and conclusion.

> How does Dickens use settings in the novel?

2) This will show the examiner that you're <u>answering the question</u>.

> Dickens uses settings in 'Great Expectations' to create symbolic meaning. The settings link to the main themes of the novel, such as crime.

The first line of the introduction gives a clear answer, which will lead on to the rest of the essay.

3) This will also help you keep the question <u>fresh in your mind</u> so your answer doesn't <u>wander off-topic</u>.

I've come to the conclusion that I really like pie...

To conclude, the introduction eases the examiner in gently, whilst the conclusion is your last chance to impress. But remember — the examiner doesn't want to see any new points lurking in those closing sentences.

Writing Main Paragraphs

So we've covered the beginning and the end, now it's time for the meaty bit. The roast beef in between the prawn cocktail and the treacle tart. This page is about how to structure your paragraphs. It's quite simple...

P.E.E.D. is how to put your argument together

Remember to start a new paragraph every time you make a new point.

1) P.E.E.D. stands for: Point, Example, Explain, Develop.

2) Begin each paragraph by making a point. Then give an example from the text (either a quote or a description). Next, explain how your example backs up your point.

3) Finally, try to develop your point by writing about its effect on the reader, how it links to another part of the text or what the writer's intention is in including it.

Use short quotes to support your ideas

1) Don't just use words from the novel to show what happens in the plot...

> Biddy cares about Pip. Pip says: "Biddy had a deep concern in everything I told her".

This just gives an example from the text without offering any explanation or analysis.

2) Instead, it's much better to use short quotes as evidence to support a point you're making.

3) It makes the essay structure clearer and smoother if most quotes are embedded in your sentences.

It's better to use short, embedded quotes as evidence. Then you can go on to explain them.

> Biddy has a "deep concern" for Pip, which suggests how much she cares about him and is interested in his troubles. Her concern also shows her caring personality, which is developed later in the novel when she cares for Mrs Joe.

Get to know some literary language

1) Using literary terms in your answer will make your essay stand out — as long as you use them correctly.

2) When you're revising, think about literary terms that are relevant to the text and how you might include them in an essay. Take a look at the table below for some examples.

Literary Term	Definition	Example
Metaphor	Describing something by saying it is something else.	"I was a steel beam of a vast engine, clashing and whirling"
Simile	Compares one thing to another, often using 'like' or 'as'.	Estella's light is "like a star."
Personification	A figure of speech that talks about a thing as if it's a person.	"The closet whispered, the fireplace sighed"

This page is so exciting — I nearly...

Now now, let's all be grown-ups and avoid the obvious joke. It's a good way of remembering how to structure your paragraphs though. Point, Example, Explain, Develop. Simple. Maybe we could make a rap or something... anyone?

Section Six — Exam Advice

In the Exam

Keeping cool in the exam can be tricky. But if you take in all the stuff on this page, you'll soon have it down to a fine art. Then you can stroll out of that exam hall with the swagger of an essay-writing master.

Don't panic if you make a mistake

1) Okay, so say you've timed the exam beautifully. Instead of putting your feet up on the desk for the last 5 minutes, it's a good idea to read through your answers and correct any mistakes...

2) If you want to get rid of a mistake, cross it out. Don't scribble it out as this can look messy. Make any corrections neatly and clearly instead of writing on top of the words you've already written.

The author uses various literary ~~teknikues~~ techniques to explore this theme .

This is the clearest way to correct a mistake. Don't be tempted to try writing on top of the original word.

3) If you've left out a word or a phrase and you've got space to add it in above the line it's missing from, write the missing bit above the line with a '∧' to show exactly where it should go.

Re-read the sentence carefully to work out where the '∧' symbol needs to go.

The writer uses imagery to draw attention to this point.
and hyperbole ∧

4) If you've left out whole sentences or paragraphs, write them in a separate section at the end of the essay. Put a star (*) next to both the extra writing and the place you want it to go.

Always keep an eye on the time

1) It's surprisingly easy to run out of time in exams. You've got to leave enough time to answer all the questions you're asked to do. You've also got to leave enough time to finish each essay properly — with a clear ending.

2) Here are some tips on how to avoid running out of time:

- Work out how much time you have for each part of your answer before you start.

- Take off a few minutes at the beginning to plan, and a few minutes at the end for your conclusion.

- Make sure you have a watch to time yourself — and keep checking it.

- Be strict with yourself — if you spend too long on one part of your answer, you may run out of time.

- If you're running out of time, keep calm, finish the point you're on and move on to your conclusion.

Stephanie never had a problem with keeping cool.

Treat an exam like a spa day — just relax...

Some people actually do lose the plot when they get into the exam. The trick is to keep calm and well... carry on. If you make sure you get your exam technique sorted, you'll be as relaxed as a sloth in a room full of easy chairs.

Sample Exam Question

Now you've had a look at how to plan and structure your answer, it's time to see an example of how it can be done. The next three pages contain loads of useful bits and bobs like the very spidery spider diagram below.

Here's a sample exam question

Read this feisty exam question. That's the best way to start...

In the exam, you'd be given the full extract in the exam paper.

Read the question carefully. Underline the important bits.

You could think about context — how social class was thought about in the Victorian era.

You'll need to discuss the passage given in detail, but you also need to refer to the rest of the book.

Q1 In Chapter Eight, read the section that begins "He calls the knaves, Jacks..." and ends "play the game out."

Beginning with this passage, write about how Dickens presents the idea of social class through the character of Pip.

Don't just write about social class in general. Write about Pip's attitudes and experiences.

Think about Dickens' use of language and characterisation.

Here's how you could plan your answer...

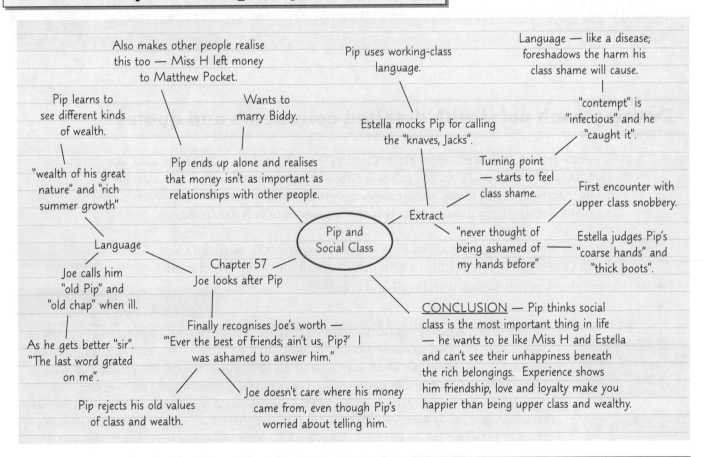

What do examiners eat? Why, egg-sam-wiches of course...

The most important thing to remember is DON'T PANIC. Take a deep breath, read the question, read it again, write a plan... take another deep breath... and then start writing. Leave about five minutes at the end to check your work too.

Worked Answer

These pages will show you how to turn an OK answer into a really good one that will impress the examiner.

Use your introduction to get off to a good start

These pages are all about how to word your sentences to impress the examiner — we haven't included everything from the plan on page 67.

You might start with something like...

> Pip's attitude towards social class is typical of the early 19th century. He wants to improve himself and doesn't seem to realise that there are more important things in life than money.

1) This intro is okay. It describes the character's attitude and also refers to the historical context.
2) Use the key words from the question to give your essay focus, and to show the examiner you're on track and that you're thinking about the question from the start.
3) But there's still room for improvement — here's a better introduction...

This shows that you understand the historical context by explaining why attitudes to social class were changing in the 19th century.

When the question asks you how a theme is explored, it's a good idea to discuss how it changes through the novel and the different viewpoints.

> Dickens uses Pip's character to show how many people in nineteenth century Britain valued wealth and social status too highly. Following the Industrial Revolution, a working class man had the chance to make a fortune and climb the social ladder, and this became the goal for many. At first Pip thinks social class is more important than family and friends, but eventually his attitude changes. Through Pip's mistakes and unhappiness, Dickens demonstrates how pointless it can be to seek wealth at the expense of other more important things.

This tells the examiner that you've thought about what message Dickens is trying to give in the novel.

Develop each point with detailed comments and quotes

> In Chapter 8, Pip meets upper class Estella for the first time. She treats him with "disdain" and makes Pip feel ashamed about his "coarse hands" and "thick boots". In Victorian times, it was really important to speak in a certain way and wear the right clothing. Pip decides after this that he wants to be a gentleman.

1) This paragraph gives many points about Pip's negative experiences of social class. But it doesn't develop the points fully or give details about any writer's techniques.
2) You should develop your points with detail and comments:

This focuses the essay on Pip's attitude to social class, instead of discussing social class in general.

It's good to develop your points by backing them up with detailed examples.

Show that you understand the novel's structure, and its significant events.

> Estella's treatment of Pip in the extract is the first time Pip feels ashamed of his lower class. Estella's criticisms of shallow things such as Pip's speech and clothes persuade Pip that appearances are what matter most in life. For example, she points out his "coarse hands" and "thick boots", which makes Pip feel ashamed. Pip's reaction to Estella's criticisms foreshadows his behaviour for much of the rest of the novel. From this moment on, he has "caught" her "infectious" disdain, and he starts to feel class shame. Dickens' language here suggests how Pip's obsession with social class will spread to all parts of his life, hurting him and his friends and family.

Referring back to the question keeps your answer focused.

Worked Answer

You need to make a variety of points

After you've explained Pip's first experience of social class and how it affects him, you could say this:

> By chapter 57 Pip's experiences have made him realise his mistakes and he is no longer interested in climbing the social ladder. Joe's kindness helps Pip realise how wrong he was to ignore Joe and Biddy.

1) This paragraph <u>introduces</u> the idea that Pip's attitude to social class <u>changes</u> through the novel.

2) However, you can improve it by discussing <u>how</u> Dickens uses <u>language</u> to emphasise Pip's new attitude:

> Explaining the effects of the language shows the examiner that you've thought about what Dickens was trying to achieve.

> In chapter 57, Pip looks at Joe and sees "the wealth of his great nature". He looks at the countryside and sees "rich summer growth". The words "wealth" and "rich" show how his point of view is changing. He realises that there are better kinds of wealth and richness than the superficial life of a gentleman that he was aiming for. Pip also describes himself "like a child". This suggests that he's beginning a new life, as someone who is a gentleman because he is kind and moral, rather than a gentleman in terms of social class and wealth.

> Don't forget to explain how your points link to the exam question.

3) Don't forget to focus on characterisation — don't talk about the characters as if they're real people.

> Dickens develops Pip's character by contrasting his changing behaviour and opinions as the novel progresses. His feelings and behaviour towards Joe are very different as a boy and as a man. When he first learns to care about social class, he angrily blames Joe for teaching him "to call those picture-cards Jacks". But when Pip learns to appreciate Joe's generosity and loyalty, he realises that if Joe felt awkward or unsure of Pip's friendship then "the fault of it was all mine".

> Mentioning Dickens' techniques shows you're aware that Pip is a fictional character, and you're discussing how he has been portrayed through language and other techniques.

Finish your essay in style

You could say:

> In conclusion, when Pip values social class over everything else, it brings darkness and unhappiness. Dickens is showing his readers that money isn't everything and that people and friends are more important.

1) This conclusion is okay but it doesn't give much <u>detail</u>, or mention any other <u>interpretations</u> of how Dickens uses Pip in his exploration of social class.

2) So to make it really <u>impressive</u> you could say something like...

> In this extract from the beginning of the novel, Pip thinks social status is important. He is ashamed of himself because he has working class clothes and speech. Later in the novel, Pip is angry because of his lack of kindness towards Joe and Biddy. This shows that he has learnt that friendship and loyalty are more important than wealth or social status. Dickens' message is not as simplistic as saying that wanting to be rich makes you a bad person. He is challenging the commonly-held idea of the time that being rich will always make you happy, and forcing both Pip and the reader to reconsider what's important in life.

> Make your last sentence really stand out — it's your last chance to impress the examiner.

Why do alligators write good essays? Their quotes are so snappy...

It seems like there's a lot to remember on these two pages, but there's not really. To summarise — write a scorching intro and a sizzling conclusion, make a good range of points (one per paragraph) and include plenty of examples. Easy.

Index

The Characters in 'Great Expectations'

Phew! You should be an expert on *Great Expectations* by now. But if you want a bit of light relief and a quick recap of what happens in the novel, sit yourself down and read through *Great Expectations — The Cartoon...*

Charles Dickens' 'Great Expectations'